ZOO CLUES

"If a trip to the zoo spells 'action' for a child you know, *Zoo Clues* is the perfect companion . . . Four sections of creatures discuss reptiles, birds, mammals, and primates. Within each section, each illustrated with droll black-line drawings, are the following features: 'Veterinarian's Behind-the-Scenes Info,' general statistics about each animal, and a 'looking at' of facts of the animal bound to captivate zoo-goers of all ages . . . Even if a trip to the zoo is only in an armchair, this volume offers great summertime reading."

—*Chicago Sun-Times*

ZOO CLUES

Making the Most of Your Visit to the Zoo

by Sheldon L. Gerstenfeld, V.M.D.

Illustrated by Eldon C. Doty

PUFFIN BOOKS

PUFFIN BOOKS
Published by the Penguin Group
Penguin Books USA Inc., 375 Hudson Street, New York, New York 10014, U.S.A.
Penguin Books Ltd, 27 Wrights Lane, London W8 5TZ, England
Penguin Books Australia Ltd, Ringwood, Victoria, Australia
Penguin Books Canada Ltd, 10 Alcorn Avenue, Toronto, Ontario, Canada M4V 3B2
Penguin Books (N.Z.) Ltd, 182–190 Wairau Road, Auckland 10, New Zealand

Penguin Books Ltd, Registered Offices: Harmondsworth, Middlesex, England

First published in the United States of America by Viking Penguin,
a division of Penguin Books USA Inc., 1991
Published in Puffin Books, 1993

3 5 7 9 10 8 6 4 2

LIBRARY OF CONGRESS CATALOGING-IN-PUBLICATION DATA
Gerstenfeld, Sheldon L., 1943–
Zoo clues: making the most of your visit to the zoo / by Sheldon
L. Gerstenfeld; illustrated by Eldon C. Doty.   p.   cm.
Summary: Text and cartoon illustrations present information about
the physical characteristics, environment, social behavior, and diet
of over thirty animals found in many zoos.
ISBN 0-14-032813-0
1. Zoo animals—Miscellanea—Juvenile literature. [1. Zoo
animals. 2. Animals. 3. Zoos.] T. Doty, Eldon. ill. II. Title.
QL775.G47 1993   92-44460 591—dc20   CIP   AC

Printed in the United States of America.
Set in ITC Bookman

Special thanks to Jerry Ward and associates for the "Zoo Shop" and "Zoo Food"
information; the American Association of Zoological Parks and Aquariums for
"Zoo Facts"; Barbara Toddes, nutritionist at the Philadelphia Zoo, for "Some
Food that the Philadelphia Zoo Buys"; Jim Joiner, bear keeper at the San Diego
Zoo, for "Cooking Lessons."

For my dear son, Tyler . . . my favorite zoo partner.

S. L. G.

CONTENTS

ACKNOWLEDGMENTS

Those individuals who devote their lives to the caring, healing, and saving of our earth's animals are some of my favorite people. Dr. Wilbur Amand, of the Philadelphia Zoo, introduced me to the fascinating world of bird and exotic medicine when I was student at the University of Pennsylvania Veterinary School, and he continues to be an inspiration. Al Porta, my favorite zookeeper, is a walking storybook of animal experiences and habits. He is a very kind and sharing person to zoo visitors and to the animals in his care. The staff at the Philadelphia Zoo has always been helpful with providing me with resources or information in writing this book or treating an animal in my hospital.

My parents, Sidney and Isabelle, nurtured and encouraged my childhood fascination for animals. Joe the Turtle, Squeaky the Duck, Butch the Fox Terrier, and my unnamed chameleon shared many of my childhood hours. My wife, Traudi, my agent, Claire M. Smith, and my editor, Deborah Brodie, have been very important in guiding the manuscript to completion . . . and the birth of this book would not have occurred without my dear son, Tyler — the kindest person I have ever known. His wonder, curiosity, and reverence for all life planted the seed for this book. I hope that *Zoo Clues* inspires many generations of parents and their children as it has done for my son and me.

S. L. G

INTRODUCTION

When my son, Tyler, was six months old, he lifted his little head and smiled at one of our house cats. Wow, I thought, if he loved seeing our cat, he'll just love the big cats. I bundled him up and took him to the zoo to see the lions and tigers. Thus began my son's and my love affair with the zoo animals. It has given us a wonderful activity to share as father and son.

Over the years, my son and I have learned as much as we could about the animals, their natural environment, their special skills and adaptations, and how we can help preserve wildlife and their environment for future generations. Our trips to the zoo have been fun, as well as a learning experience.

To help your children get the most from their visit, read *Zoo Clues* before going to the zoo. You may want to spend time at only a few exhibits (just reptiles or a few mammals). To help your children get the most from their visit, let them linger over their favorite animal — the elephants, for example. Look at the elephant's body language, listen to the sounds they make. Use all your senses. Ask your kids thought-provoking questions: Which elephant seems to be the boss? Do they seem to have individual personalities? Try to leave the zoo with more information about animals and wildlife conservation than you had when you entered. By the year 2000 approximately 600,000 species of plants and animals may be extinct. Every one of us has a responsibility to make sure that we do all we can to ensure that our children are not the last generation to see many of these animals and to prevent animals from showing up on the endangered species list in the first place.

A trip to the zoo should be more than making a "monkey" out of ourselves. I hope that this book will allow parents and their children to share and delight in the reverence for all animal life — just as it has done for my son and me. Read this book before your zoo trip. Take it along when you visit our animal friends. The way you experience the animal world will never be the same again.

Sheldon L. Gerstenfeld
V.M.D.

ZOO CLUES

Reptiles

Reptiles are cold-blooded, horny-scaled, or bony- plated animals with backbones. They never have hair, feathers, or mammary glands (breasts). Cold-blooded animals depend on the environment for their body temperatures: they cannot regulate their own. Reptiles give birth to live young or lay leathery-skinned eggs.

Alligators and Crocodiles

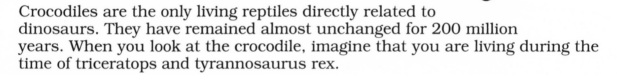

Gators and crocs are the largest reptiles in the world. They are cold–blooded animals that have scaly skin, breathe with lungs, and lay eggs. The cold-blooded animal depends on the outside temperature to "set" its body temperature inside.

Spanish explorers visiting Florida named the strange-looking reptile "El Legarto" — "The Lizard." "El Legarto" became "alligator."

Crocodiles are the only living reptiles directly related to dinosaurs. They have remained almost unchanged for 200 million years. When you look at the crocodile, imagine that you are living during the time of triceratops and tyrannosaurus rex.

Looking at Alligators and Crocodiles

Eyes and Nostrils

The eyes and nostrils are perfectly placed on top of the head so they can see and breathe while the rest of the their body is underwater. Great for sneak attacks — or is that snack attacks?

Jaws

Do you think that a human can hold a gator or croc's jaw shut? Yes. They have huge muscles to close their mouths, but very weak muscles to open them. So a human can keep the mouth shut — the hard part is getting close enough to shut it!

smooth   scales

Tail

Their muscular tail is used for swimming or as a powerful whiplike weapon.

Skin

On the back, the tough, leathery scales have ridges, but on the belly, they are smooth. If you can't see the smooth belly don't roll him over . . . just take my word that it is smooth! There are no sweat glands.

3

Teeth

It is fortunate that they don't
need to brush their teeth because
they have at least 60 sharp teeth.
They have spare teeth under their gum line
ready to take the place of broken or worn-out teeth.
In fact, they may go through a few thousand
pearly-white teeth in a lifetime.

crocodile   **alligator**

Are you looking at an alligator or crocodile?

Crocodiles have a long, triangle-shaped head and
all the teeth (top and bottom) can be seen on the
outside of the mouth. Alligators have a flat, broad
head and, when they close their mouths, you will
see only the top teeth.

Keeping Cool, Reptile-Style

Since they are cold-
blooded, their body
temperature depends
on the surrounding air
and water temperature.
During the day, crocs
and gators keep cool by
going into the water.
You may also see them
lying on land with
their mouths wide
open, panting like a
dog, or seeking out
shady spots.

Lounge Lizards in the Sun

Reptiles keep warm by basking in the sunlight. Also, they take an evening soak after the water warms up during the day.

Alligator and Crocodile Stats

Temperature Preferred:
90-95° F

Eggs Incubated:
60-70 days

Life Span:
30-40 years

Veterinarians'

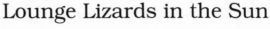

Behind the Scenes
Info

• They hiss, snap their jaws, and lash with their tail when angry.

• A medium-sized alligator can knock an adult down.

• In the zoo, alligators and crocodiles are fed a mixture of whole animals — chickens, rats, pigeons, or fish.

• Alligators and crocodiles tend to get fat, so their weight and the amount of food they eat is monitored weekly.

• It is difficult to tell which is the boy or girl alligator or crocodile but during the mating season it is easy . . . the male is more aggressive and noisy.

• In humans, stitches are removed in one week, but reptile skin heals more slowly. Stitches are removed in four weeks.

Turtles and Tortoises

Humans are the new kid on the block. We've been on earth only a few thousand years. Turtles have been around for 200 million years! Turtles seem to have great wisdom — move slowly and surely, be peaceful, and you will reach your goals. Should humans listen to the "voice of the turtle?"

Looking at Turtles

Shell

You will know if the turtle lives on land or water by the shape of the shell. A high-domed model means "I live on land." Freshwater and sea turtles have flat shells. The shell is not dead weight. It is a living, breathing structure. When weighing turtles for medication, the weight of the living shell is included.

Feet and Legs

Tortoises have thick, heavy legs for walking on land. Thick, heavy scales protect the front legs. Tortoises have four toes on the back foot. Freshwater turtles have webbed feet with five toes on the back foot. Sea turtles have flat, oarlike flippers.

The Turtle Restaurant — Zoo Style

Tortoises dine on flowers, cactus, grass, Swiss chard, cucumbers, thawed frozen mixed vegetables, fresh fruit, melons, and a small amount of bread and dog food. In the desert, tortoises get their water from cactus. Freshwater turtles and terrapins eat earthworms, fish, green leafy vegetation (watercress and Swiss chard), and some dog food.

Note: If you have a pet turtle, keep it on a well-balanced diet. Always talk to your veterinarian before purchasing a turtle — or any pet — and have it examined by your veterinarian.

Ear

They don't have earlobes like we do, but they do have an eardrum covered by scales located below and behind the eye.

Mouth

Turtles and tortoises have a toothless, horny beak like birds. It is a perfect tool for tearing and crushing.

Watch the Turtle Eat

The head and neck can be pulled strongly backward (retracted). This helps the turtle tear its food apart. Watch the turtle push the food away with its front legs while pulling on it with its head.

How does a hot turtle get cool?

By burrowing in dirt or sand, going in the water, or finding a shady area. Its skin does not have sweat glands.

Watch the Tortoises and Turtles Drink Water

They dip their snouts in water and take it in by suction.

Turtle Dating

A male turtle shows that he is in love with a female turtle by grunting, gently biting, or butting her. The male water turtle may stroke his girlfriend with the long fingernails on his front legs while swimming.

Veterinarians' Behind the Scenes Info

- If a blood sample is needed from a 600 lb. Galapagos or Aldabra tortoise, the jugular vein (in the neck) is used or a claw is clipped short.

- To radiograph (X–ray) a turtle, it is placed on the table with head and legs extended. The X-ray beam is directed through the shell.

- If a pregnant turtle has difficulty delivering her eggs, a Caesarean can be done. She is anesthetized with gas anesthesia. A high-speed orthopedic or dental drill cuts a hole in the bottom shell (plastron). The eggs are removed from the uterus and the shell is put back in place with fiberglass and epoxy resin.

Turtle Stats

Speed:
1/5 mile (about 1,000 feet) in one hour — measure the distance

Heart Rate:
20-30 beats per minute (What is your heart rate?)

Best Temp.:
80-85° F

Snakes

Snakes scare many people but you will find, as you get to know them, that they are among the most fascinating and beautiful creatures on earth. You may even start to love them.

There are about 3,000 different kinds of snakes. Only about 200 are poisonous to humans. Even the venomous snakes will not go out of their way to harm you. They are shy creatures that bite only if bothered.

You'll find as many snakes in Antarctica as penguins in the Sahara desert — none. Snakes are found on all continents except Antarctica.

Looking at Snakes

Skin

Compare the scale patterns of the different snakes. Can you identify a snake by its pattern? Are the scales on its back shaped differently from those on its belly?

Tongue

Snakes are not "tongue-tied." They smell and taste by flicking their tongue in and out. Small dust specks are carried into the mouth to a taste "computer" called Jacobson's Organs — located on the roof of the mouth. What if we had Jacobson's Organs?

Imitate a snake. We probably look silly to snakes because we don't flick our tongues.

Watch the Snake Move

Snakes walk with their ribs. On the snake's belly is a series of large plates called *scutes*. Each is free at the rear edge and attached at the front edge to a movable rib. The ribs and plates are moved forward and backward as the snake "digs in" and moves along.

Snakes may also push off against rocks, sticks, and other objects as they wiggle their bodies from side to side.

The rattlesnake known as the sidewinder can "walk" across the desert by somersaulting through the loose sand.

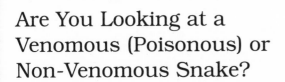

Are You Looking at a Venomous (Poisonous) or Non-Venomous Snake?

Poisonous snakes have two long teeth called fangs, one on each side in the upper jaw. The other teeth are shorter. The large fangs are found more frequently in the front of the mouth but there are rear-fanged snakes, such as the African boomslang.

The poison is delivered from venom glands in the side of the head through hollow or channeled fangs.

Snake Stats

Life Span

Garter snake: 5-7 years

King cobra: 10-15 years

Reticulated python:
20-25 years

Diamondback
rattlesnake:
20-25 years

Anaconda: 20-30 years

Indian python:
30-35 years

Boa: 30-40 years

Longest
(non-poisonous)

Anaconda: 37 feet

Reticulated python:
32 feet

Longest (poisonous)

King cobra: 18 feet

Eastern diamondback
rattlesnake U.S.: 6 feet

Shortest

Thread snake:
4 1/2 inches

Heaviest
(non-poisonous)

Anaconda: 500 lbs.

Heaviest (poisonous)

Eastern diamondback
rattlesnake: 34 lbs.

Fastest

Black mamba:
5-12 m.p.h.

Coachwhip/red racer:
3 1/2 m.p.h.

Birds

Birds are warm-
blooded, feathered,
egg-laying animals with
backbones. Animals
with backbones are
called vertebrates.
Worms and insects do
not have backbones
and are called inverte-
brates. Not all birds fly.
Penguins can't, but
they're great swimmers
and divers.

Owls

Owls look smart and wise. In fact, they always seem to have a question that's never answered: "Who? Who?"

The owl is the fast-food champion of the night sky. With the help of remarkable eyes, hearing, and sharp claws, the owl swiftly and quietly swoops down on its evening "carry-out" meal — rodents, birds, and insects. Although most are nocturnal, some, like the great gray owl, are day hunters.

Looking at Owls

Head

An owl's head can be turned quickly in a complete circle. Turn your head to the left and to the right. See how limited your sight is without turning your body.

Beak

An owl's beak is sharp enough to tear meat.

Claws

These eight talons are like sharp, curved hooks. The prey rarely escapes.

Ears

An owl doesn't have earlobes. It would lose too much body heat through them; also, the lobes would add too much weight to a bird that must fly quietly and swiftly. Owls have large holes for ear openings under feathers behind the eyes. They can hear a mouse walking more than fifty feet away.

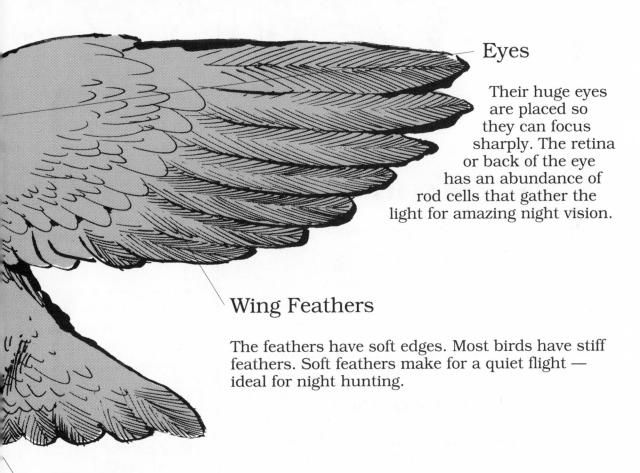

Eyes

Their huge eyes are placed so they can focus sharply. The retina or back of the eye has an abundance of rod cells that gather the light for amazing night vision.

Wing Feathers

The feathers have soft edges. Most birds have stiff feathers. Soft feathers make for a quiet flight — ideal for night hunting.

Leg Feathers

The leg feathers are like knights' armor. They help protect the owl from being bitten by its "meals."

Do you see any owl droppings?

Owl droppings are called pellets. Unlike hawks and falcons, owls cannot digest the bones, teeth, and hair of their nighttime meals. When you hike in woods, look for owl pellets near the base of trees and you will discover an owl's home.

How can you tell if owls are angry?

They spread their wings, fluff up their feathers, and hiss.

Owl Stats

Weight - Elf owl: 45 grams
Pygmy owl: 155 grams
Great horned owl: 1450 grams
Snowy owl: 2020 grams

Heart Rate: 200-300 beats per minute

Breathing Rate: 15-25 breaths per minute (count them)

Number of eggs (clutch): 2-8

Sit on Eggs (incubation): Pygmy: 24 days
Snowy and Great horned: 34 days

Leave the Nest (to fledge): about 8 weeks

Life Span: 20-25 years

Veterinarians' Behind the Scenes Info

• The talons can injure humans, so leather gloves may be used when holding an owl.

• In the zoo, owls are fed whole rodents, birds, or fish, or they may be fed a commercial bird-of–prey diet.

Ostriches

The ostrich is the largest bird in the world. Ostriches share watering holes, peacefully, with antelopes, zebras, and wild cattle from the Arabian and Sahara deserts and throughout the sandy plains of Africa. Ostriches like to live in groups of twenty or thirty feathered friends.

Looking at Ostriches

Beak

Ostriches do not have teeth. The beak is too soft to use for defense — but it is a perfect structure for eating their favorite foods — insects, frogs, lizards, snakes, mice, grasses, and bushes. Yummy. The beak is also a handy tool for turning the ostrich eggs.

Wings

Ostriches cannot fly. They use their small wings for balance while running.

Feet

Ostriches have one large toe and one small toe (in the same family, called *ratites*). *Cassowaries, emus,* and *rheas* have three large toes. The "heel" is two to three feet off the ground - perfectly made for fast, powerful running and kicking.

Can you speak Ostrich?

"Boo Boo Boo Hoo" means "I love you." (The male ostriches' call during the mating season).

"Hiss": "I'm angry."

Ostrich Body Language

When a male fans his tail and wing feathers to other males, he is showing anger. If he displays tail and wing feathers to a female, especially while dancing and swaying his head, it means "I love you."

Watch the Ostrich Bathe

Ostriches don't swim or bathe in water. They take dust baths. We could call this a "dry shampoo!"

REGULAR OLD Dirt

"Egg-citing" Information

• 8 eggs are usually laid in an 8-foot nest dug in the sand.

• The parents turn the eggs by wiggling their bodies or using their beaks.

• The chick pips while in the shell — makes sounds and uses its egg tooth (a small projection on the beak). "Pipping" stimulates all the chicks to hatch at the same time. This is definitely an advantage in the wild, since the male leads the chicks away from the nest one day after hatching. A late hatcher may be left behind and preyed on by snakes, buzzards, and other animals.

• The chicks usually break out of the thick-shelled egg with a karate kick from their powerful legs. In a few hours, they are ready to stand.

KARATE CHICK

Veterinarians' Behind the Scenes Info

• An ostrich can only kick *forward* —a good thing to know if you are the veterinarian or keeper.

• The ostrich, in general, is a very hardy and healthy bird, but if they do get sick, they eat less, fluff up, are sleepy, quiet, and may have diarrhea.

• Ostriches *do not* bury their head in the sand when frightened — they run *fast* when scared. This story probably began because ostriches have their heads flat on the ground a lot while they are feeding and, from a distance, the pipelike neck seems to disappear into the ground.

• Ostriches are tough birds and can be very aggressive, especially during the mating season.

• How do you move an ostrich? With baffleboards — padded plywood boards that protect the handlers from powerful ostrich kicks. Experienced handlers can place a hood over the ostrich's head (to quiet the bird), stand on each side of the bird, grasp the wings, and press down on its back so it can't jump up and kick.

• Ostriches swallow pebbles that stay in their stomach and help grind up food.

• In the zoo, they are fed the "ratite diet" — Zu/Preem or combinations of turkey pellets, kale and other greens, and dry dog food. Crickets and mealworms are good "busy food" for ostriches. They like searching for these insect snacks.

Ostrich Stats

Height: 8 feet

Weight: 300 lbs.

Sexually Mature: 2 years old

Weight of Egg: 2-3 lbs.

Incubation Period: 45 days

Parrots

Parrots are loved for their extraordinary beauty, brilliant rainbow of colors, and their ability to mimic the human voice. Recently, parrots have been found to name objects and their color and shape by use of symbols. Also, by the use of symbols or vocalization (speaking), they have been able to tell if objects are the "same" or "different." Parrots are not mindless mimics but, as we are discovering, intelligent . . . definitely not "bird brains." This is why it is important for zoo birds and your pet birds to have a lot of mental stimulation — toys and social interaction. Dr. Irene Pepperberg and her wonderful parrot Alex have been the pioneers in bird–human communication.

There are more than 300 different species of parrots. They are found in the tropics on all lands of the southern hemisphere, except the southern tip of Africa and a few Pacific islands. Some parrots call Arizona and New Mexico home.

Looking at Parrots

Beak

Parrots are called "hookbills." The huge, curved beak and thick tongue are well suited for cracking nuts and large seeds and scooping the kernel from the shell. Also, parrots climb by using their beak like an extra hand.

Feathers

Most parrots are brightly colored — ideal camouflage in tropical forests. The feathers protect the body and are important for flying. Feathers also have other functions: they can signal sexual or aggressive displays (witness the cockatoo showing off its head crest). Look at the pattern and color of a parrot's feathers. Each species has its own "school colors."

Ears

Are you having a hard time finding the parrot's ears? It doesn't have earlobes like humans. Earlobes would weigh too much. Also, birds must save heat to maintain their high body temperature. A lot of heat is lost from our earlobes. The bird's small ear canal is located slightly behind and below the eye, covered by feathers.

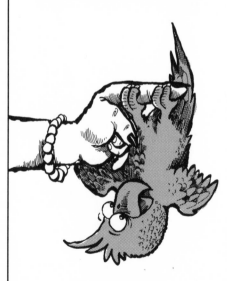

Feet and Legs

The scales are a remnant of the reptile heritage of all birds. They serve as protective leg armor. Parrots can bring food up to their mouths with their feet. Two toes point forward and two point backward, giving the parrot a very strong "toe-hold" for gripping slippery food, climbing, or just hanging upside down.

Do parrots ever "fall out of bed" when they are sleeping?

The parrot's foot locks on the branch while the bird sleeps, so it never falls from tree branches or perches.

Preen and Clean

Watch the birds preen. Birds spend many hours preening — making themselves look pretty. Preening involves using the beak to reattach separated barbs on the feathers and to put the feathers back in position. Birds also like to preen each other. This is the bird equivalent of tenderness — "running your fingers through someone's hair." Most parrots have a preen gland near the tail base. When the parrot preens, it may distribute the oil from the preen gland onto its feathers to help waterproof them and keep them healthy. By the way, Amazon parrots don't have a preen gland.

The "Scoop" on Parrot Droppings

Look at the parrot's droppings. Parrots do not have a "storage tank," or urinary bladder, like humans. (All that water would make flying difficult). The white, solid part of the targetlike droppings is from the urinary system. The dark green wastes from the digestive system are also excreted. The food passes through the parrot's digestive system in three hours. In humans, passage is about twelve hours.

Parrot Stats

Heart Rate: 150-300 beats per minute

Flight Speed: 25-40 m.p.h.

Healthy Droppings: 30 per day

Life Span: 60-70 years (Amazons, African Greys, macaws, and cockatoos)

Swans

Swans are beautiful and graceful. The Mute swan is a large bird with an orange beak that has a black nail at the tip. The base of the beak (near the nostrils) has a black bump. They are quiet birds in contrast to their more vocal cousins, the Whooper, Whistling, Bewick, and Trumpeter swans.

Australia and New Zealand are home to Black swans. In the wild, you may see 25,000 to 50,000 in a flock! The Black-necked and Coscoroba swans are found in South America.

Swans eat plants from the bottom of ponds, lakes, rivers, and estuaries (an area where the ocean meets the river). They eat insects, snails, tadpoles, and small fish for snacks. They swallow small stones to help digestion.

Swans are found in our art and literature. To "be like a swan" is to have purity, courage, and supernatural powers. The expression "swan song" means a last act or final expression before death; it refers to the myth of the swan's habit of singing before death. The beauty and grace of the swan is superbly illustrated in the ballets *Swan Lake* and *The Dying Swan*.

Looking at Swans

Beak

The beak or bill is flat to help scoop up food from the mud or water. Do you see fringes on the side of the bill? These strain out the mud and water, and help keep the food in the mouth.

Neck

The neck is the swan's outstanding feature. Its neck is longer than its body. The swan has more neckbones (23) than the long-necked giraffe (7)!

Legs

Their legs are short and set farther back than those of ducks and geese. They are great for water cruising, but awkward for land roving — true "sea legs."

Body

Swans are boat-shaped. This streamlined shape helps them move through the water.

Feet

Swans' feet are large, webbed paddles. When swans are hot, the webs get sweaty.

Can you "bob" upside down?

Swans are the bobbing champions of the world. To feed on the water bottom, a swan thrusts its head and long neck underwater and its tail bobs up.

25

How do you waterproof a swan?

Swans waterproof their feathers by rubbing their beaks on an oil gland near the tail and combing the oil through each feather. They preen (straighten out and reconnect) their feathers to keep warm and dry and to look pretty.

Grounded for Repairs

Swans molt or shed their feathers once a year, usually after mating. The flight or large wing feathers are shed (fall out) together. The swans are grounded until new flight feathers grow in.

• Male swans will fight to protect their territory after finding a mate.

• When swans "fall in love," they have a fascinating "wedding" ceremony called the *nuptial*

display. They dip and stretch their necks toward each other, move their heads from side to side, rub their necks, and "kiss." Their large wings flap back and forth like giant fans. The cob (male) mounts the pen (female) and fertilizes the eggs inside the female's body.

• The cob and pen usually stay together for life.

• Mother and father swans are wonderful parents so the zoo staff leaves them alone to rear their own young.

• Their grass and plant nests are ten feet across and three feet deep. This protects baby swans, called cygnets, from the water and from predators (foxes, wolves, coyotes, otters, and gulls).

• Both parents share egg sitting (incubation).

• Baby swans (cygnets) hatch in 35 days. They have grayish-brown feathers for one year. They fledge (leave the nest) at four months.

Veterinarians' Behind the Scenes Info

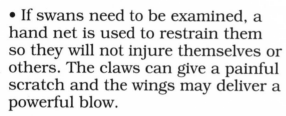

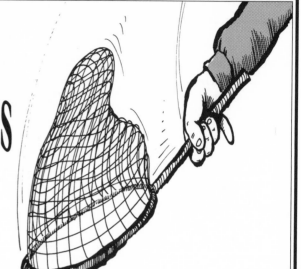

• If swans need to be examined, a hand net is used to restrain them so they will not injure themselves or others. The claws can give a painful scratch and the wings may deliver a powerful blow.

• In the zoo, swans are fed game-bird chow, trout chow, greens in or on the water (lettuce, sprouted wheat), and grass. A quartzite grit is fed to help grind up food in a part of the stomach called the gizzard.

• The young cygnets are watched carefully during the first few weeks of life since they are sometimes slow in learning food-gathering skills and may die of starvation unless helped.

Swan Stats

Height:
5 feet (Trumpeter swan with neck extended)

Weight:
30 lbs. (Mute swan)
35 lbs. (Trumpeter)

Wingspread:
8-10 feet (Trumpeter)

Flight Speed:
50-75 m.p.h.

Life Span: 25-50 years

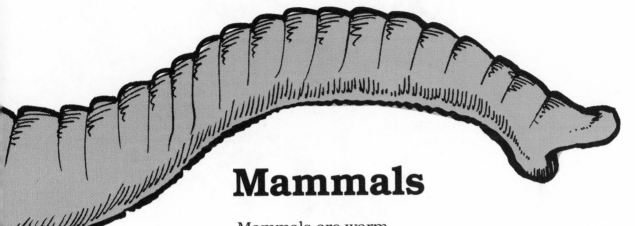

Mammals

Mammals are warm-blooded animals with a backbone. Warm-blooded animals' temperature is regulated internally and does not depend on the temperature of the environment. Hair, fur, or blubber provides insulation, and a four-chambered heart helps keep the body temperature steady. The young are nourished with milk from the mammary glands (breasts) of their mother.

Anteaters

The anteater is a comical-looking animal, but to anteaters we probably look funny. Pretend that you are an anteater and look at the zoo watchers. We have fleshy things on the side of our heads (ears) and tiny snouts . . . Pretty funny. What do you think we look like to the giraffe, camel, and other zoo animals?

Anteaters are made perfectly for what they do best. In the wild, they dine on termites, ants, beetles and their larvae, and ripe fruit. They use their powerful front legs and long claws to rip apart anthills, termite mounds, and logs to get their food. Here's a great idea: Why don't we eliminate spraying chemicals for termite control by surrounding our houses with anteaters!

The giant anteater makes its home in the swamps, rainforests, and savannahs of Central and South America.

Looking at Anteaters

Tail

The anteater's tail is nearly as long as its body. That must be a real "drag!"

Fur

Their fur is gray-black in color. They have a black diagonal "shoulder strap."

Snout and Tongue

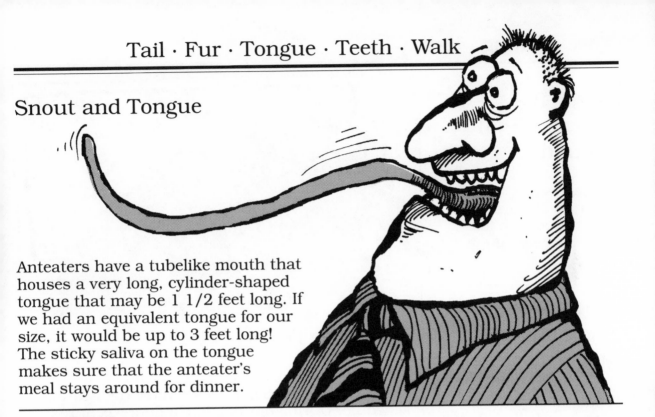

Anteaters have a tubelike mouth that houses a very long, cylinder-shaped tongue that may be 1 1/2 feet long. If we had an equivalent tongue for our size, it would be up to 3 feet long! The sticky saliva on the tongue makes sure that the anteater's meal stays around for dinner.

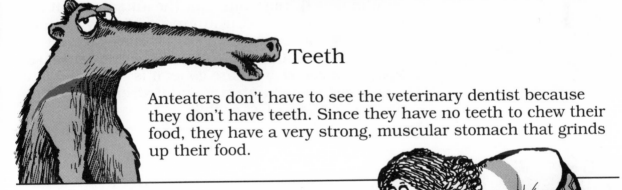

Teeth

Anteaters don't have to see the veterinary dentist because they don't have teeth. Since they have no teeth to chew their food, they have a very strong, muscular stomach that grinds up their food.

Can You Walk Like An Anteater?

You'd have to walk on your knuckles and the sides of your hands. This posture protects their long, strong claws. They shuffle when they walk, but they can gallop fast.

Watch the Anteater Sniff Around

Anteaters are "nosy." Their great sense of smell makes up for their poor hearing and eyesight.

Antburgers Are Not on the Zoo Menu

A special anteater diet in the zoo is horsemeat, mink chow, hard-boiled eggs, molasses, peanut oil, honey, vitamins, and minerals.

Nighttime Dining

Since anteaters prefer to be busy and eat at night (nocturnal), some zoos reverse the lighting schedule. During our daytime a fluorescent red light makes it "nighttime" for the anteater so it is busy eating and moving around. This way you and other zoo visitors see an active anteater. A white fluorescent light (Vita-Lite) is used for the next 12 hours. All zoo visitors are gone: it is "daytime" (our nighttime) for the anteater and it sleeps and dreams of the perfect anthill.

Anteater Housekeeping

Anteaters pick a place and deposit their wastes (urine and feces) in one area of their environment. Can you find it?

Veterinarians' Behind the Scenes Info

• Bandaging the front claws makes it easier and safer to restrain the anteater for examination.

• Anteaters don't bite since they don't have teeth.

• Obesity (getting fat) is the anteater's biggest health problem. As a rule, anteaters are very healthy animals.

• The tongue needs special care if the anteater needs anesthesia for surgery. It hangs out and gets dry, so the veterinary staff keeps it wet until the animal recovers.

Anteater Stats

Weight: 50-125 lbs.

Length:
2 1/2 feet (body)
2 1/2 feet (tail)

Body Temp.:
91.4° F (low!)

Breathing Rate:
15 breaths/minute

Gestation (pregnancy):
190 days

Number of babies: 1

Birth Weight: 2-4 lbs.

Weaning Age:
4-6 weeks

Weaning Weight: 7 lbs.

Armadillos

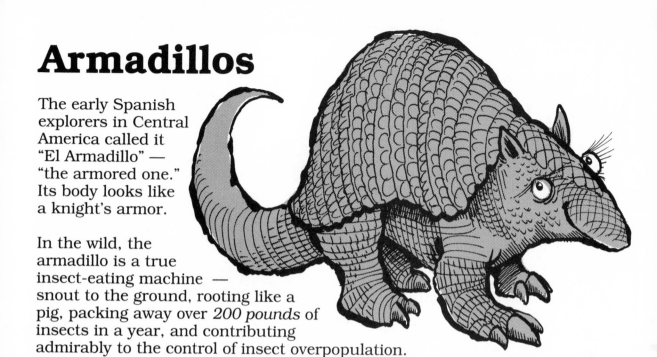

The early Spanish explorers in Central America called it "El Armadillo" — "the armored one." Its body looks like a knight's armor.

In the wild, the armadillo is a true insect-eating machine — snout to the ground, rooting like a pig, packing away over *200 pounds* of insects in a year, and contributing admirably to the control of insect overpopulation.

The armadillo is a world-class digger found only in the Americas — Southern United States, Mexico, Central and South America. In Mississippi, it is nicknamed the "grave digger."

Looking at Armadillos

Walking Armor —
Can you find the weak spot?

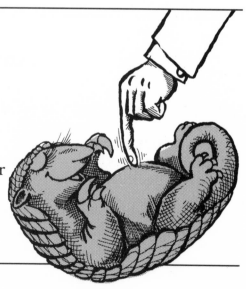

The armadillo wears a stiff, leathery wrapping. The head and rump are solid; the middle is divided into flexible bands. The flexible bands allow the armadillo to roll up into a tight ball for protection if it can't escape by digging. Where can you tickle an armadillo? On its belly. This is the only spot with no armor. It is the armadillo's area most vulnerable to attack.

Ears

The armadillo's ears look like they were borrowed from a mule.

Eyes

Armadillos should wear glasses. They don't see well. Their long eyelashes protect their eyes as they bump and dig through the underbrush.

Watch 'em Root with the Snoot or He "Nose" How to Root

The nose (snout) is a first-class rooting device that can smell insects almost a foot underground. The armadillo quickly pokes and buries the snout in the soft ground and munches on termites and other insect delights. A small snake may even be included in the dinner if it gets in the way.

Tongue

The tongue is a rapid-firing device that has wartlike projections. The sticky saliva on the tongue gets coated with insects as it's flicked into the soft ground.

Teeth

The armadillo has only molars (cheek teeth in the rear of the jaw) — 32 of them — that grow continuously. The armadillo wears them down to a comfortable size by eating roots and other hard food.

Claws

The armadillo has four claws on the front feet and five on the back feet. These thick, long, and sharp claws help make the armadillo a high-powered steam shovel that can quickly dig a den that may extend for six feet or more and ends in a three-or-four-feet-deep space where the armadillo likes to sleep during the day.

Demolition Derby, Armadillo-Style

Armadillos move around like armored bumper cars — crashing through or bumping into anything in their way.

The "Armadillo Walk" — Try It

Walk on your fingertips (claw tips) and the heels of your feet. Armadillos can outrun a human.

Listen to the Armadillo's Voice

The armadillo grunts like a pig when it roots. In fact, it is sometimes called the "poor man's pig."

The Armadillo Swim Team

Armadillos are excellent swimmers. Apparently they can swallow air and float across a pond or stream. They have a remarkable ability to hold their breath for five or even ten minutes! They have been seen walking on the bottom of ponds for six minutes without taking a breath.

What do your house cat and an armadillo have in common?

They both like to use a litter box.

Armadillo Babies

Four very small(2 ounces each) and identical young are born at the same time. None of them have hair.

The Armadillo's Zoo Menu

They are fed canned dog or cat food with some fruit and extra vitamin K.

Veterinarians' Behind the Scenes Info

• The thick shell requires a very strong X-ray machine to get a good picture (radiograph) of an organ that may be causing a medical problem.

• If an armadillo gets sore feet, zoo vets place a medicated foot bath strategically between the nesting area and the food area. The armadillo must walk through the medicine several times a day.

• If an armadillo needs surgery, injectable (with a needle) anesthesia is used, not gas, because these armored fellows can hold their breath for ten minutes and stay awake!

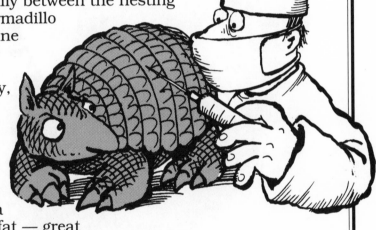

• In the zoo, armadillos have a tendency to "pig out" and get fat — great food and not enough armadillo aerobic classes.

Armadillo Stats

Weight: 10 lbs. (Nine-banded) to 130 lbs.(Giant)	**Body Temp.:** 90° F (low!)	**Litter Size:** 4-8
Body length: 2-4 feet	**Puberty:** 1 year old (able to have babies)	**Eyes Open:** 25 days
Tail length: 1-2 feet	**Pregnancy:** 260 days	**Weaning Age:** 6 weeks
		Life Span: 15 years

Sloths

The sloth is a very slow and gentle animal that lives almost entirely in the tall rainforest trees of Central and South America. Leaves, buds, fruits, and twigs are its favorite foods.

Would you like to meet relatives of the sloth that are as big as elephants?. . . You're too late. . . by 50 million years.

Looking at Sloths

Claws

The claws are used for "hooking" to trees. Although sloths are very docile, the claws can also be used for protection.

Two-Toed or Three-Toed Sloth?   The front feet will tell you.

Arms

Their arms are longer than their legs — great for tree hanging and reaching for food.

Hair Coat

The sloths have a very thick fur coat that keeps them warm if the weather gets too cold. Sloths can't shiver. Shivering helps many animals produce heat and keep warm. The thick hair coat also keeps the sloth cool in hot weather (just as it does for your dog). In the thick coat, there are air pockets that are filled with cooler air. Look at the direction of the hair. It is parted on the belly, so that water can flow off easily. As sloths hang upside down, the hair on their body and legs is pointed toward the ground for efficient shedding of water. . . the sloths' answer to "drip-drying."

Mouth

The horny lips are well adapted to the sloth's leaf, twig, bud, and fruit diet. Sloths get their permanent teeth before they are born. Their teeth grow continuously and are worn down by eating coarse foods.

Muscles

Sloths are marshmallows! 50 percent of human's body weight is muscle while 25 percent of a sloth's body weight is muscle.

The Sloth Is a Real "Tree Potato"

They literally sleep their life away. . . blowing zzzzzz's for 20 hours a day!

Hanging Around— Sloth-Style

Sloths see the world from a different perspective than we do . . . . They like to hang around, often upside down. They may ball up in the fork of a tree and look like a termite nest or a knot of a tree. Perfect camouflage!

Don't Stand Under a Tree With a Sloth in It

In the wild, they like to urinate and defecate from the treetops when it is raining, so that the animals that prey on them will not be able to hear them. Sometimes sloths will climb down to the ground, dig a hole, urinate, defecate, cover it up, and climb back to their safe haven. Everything about a sloth is slow. In fact, they may urinate or defecate only once a week. They have a very large bladder that can stretch to hold a lot of urine.

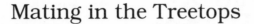

Mating in the Treetops

The female is pregnant for about six months. She gives birth to one baby that is delivered in 15 – 30 minutes while she hangs in the treetops by her arms, with her legs dangling. The baby comes out headfirst, clutches the mother's fur, and is gently grabbed by her. A baby sloth does not assume the upside-down posture of the adult until he is 12 weeks old. The mother nurses him for three months.

Is the sloth slower than a turtle?

The sloth would lose a race with a tortoise. A land speed of 10 feet per minute (600 feet per hour) is top speed for a sloth. High gear for a tortoise is 1,000 feet per hour. Sloths are masters of the tall trees but they are almost helpless on the ground. They lie flat and must drag themselves on the ground. They are most vulnerable to their enemies at this time (anacondas, ocelots, harpy eagles, and caimans). Some humans also hunt them for food. By the way, sloths are good swimmers. They can even do the backstroke — slowly!

Veterinarians'
Behind the Scenes Info

• In the zoo, sloths like to eat dog food, milk, eggs, celery, bananas, and green vegetables.

• They have been known to survive periods of not breathing from 10-40 minutes.

• In the wild, sloths have green or slimy hair coats. Algae growth! The sloth hair is a wonderful home for algae that grows in the humid rainforests. In the zoo, newly arrived sloths with algae are given weekly copper sulfate baths.

• Baby sloths have been hand-reared on an evaporated milk, water, and vitamin formula. A surrogate mother is some-times made out of a rolled Turkish towel so that the sloth will not get overly attached to humans. The babies begin to eat solid food (fruit, yogurt, bananas) when they are 8 weeks old.

Sloth Stats

Height: 2 feet

Weight: 10-20 lbs.

Body Temp.:
75° to 91° F (very low!)

Breathing Rate:
6-8 breaths/minute

Speed: 10 feet/min.
(walking on the ground)
100 feet/min.
(in the trees)

Pregnancy:
120-180 days
(Three-toed)
263 days (Two-toed)

Aardvarks

"Earth pig" (Afrikaner name), "Earth hog", "ant bear", or just "Kukukifuku" (Swahili). All are common names for the funny-looking mammal with the big body, long head, and snout ending in a piglike muzzle.

In the wild, the aardvark calls Africa, south of the Sahara desert, home, and dines on ants, termites, and insect larvae.

Looking at Aardvarks

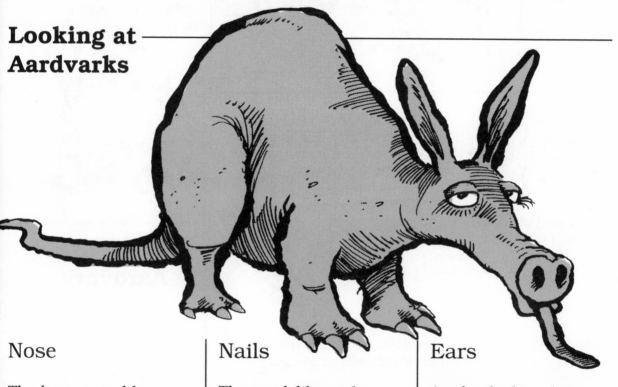

Nose

The long, movable snout is a very efficient ant and termite finder.

Nails

The spadelike nails help make the aardvark a digging champion.

Ears

Aardvarks have big ears, probably to help them hear the insects better. Watch them fold their ears back when they're digging, to keep the dirt out.

Body

Their muscular body, legs, and tail help aardvarks dig a hole faster than you can say "Kukukifuku!" In the wild, they dig burrows with many chambers. Need a hole dug fast? Rent an aardvark.

Watch the Aardvark Sleep

An aardvark likes to cover its snout with its tail and hind feet when it sleeps. Aardvarks are nocturnal animals — active and feeding at night.

Veterinarians' Behind the Scenes Info

• The aardvarks' zoo menu: dry dog food, chopped meat, eggs, milk, oatmeal, honey, vitamins, and minerals.

• How do you hold an aardvark? . . . with difficulty. They whirl around and turn somersaults when touched. They are also very strong and have sharp nails.

• Sleep chemicals are used to immobilize the aardvark, if it needs an examination or surgery.

• In general, aardvarks are healthy but sometimes they do get colds. . . a giant-sized stuffed nose!

• Aardvark babies are born wrinkled and hairless.

Aardvark Stats

Weight:
100-150 lbs.

Pregnancy:
210-240 days

Life Span:
15-20 years

Kangaroos

Kangaroos are the largest living pouched animals (marsupials). They live in the open woods, plains, arid heavy brush of Australia and Tasmania. Male kangaroos are called boomers. Females are called does and a group of 'roos is called a mob.

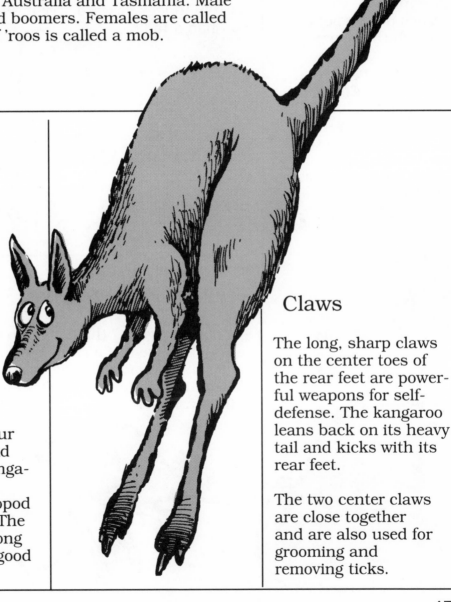

Looking at Kangaroos

Feet

Kangaroos have *long* feet. Can you find the heels? How would the lifestyle of humans have changed if we were born with feet this long? Would we hop to school? How would our sports change? How about shoes? Draw a picture of our world if humans had been made with kangaroo feet. Kangaroos belong to the macropod —"big foot" family. The foot is long and strong from heel to toe — good for leaping.

Claws

The long, sharp claws on the center toes of the rear feet are powerful weapons for self-defense. The kangaroo leans back on its heavy tail and kicks with its rear feet.

The two center claws are close together and are also used for grooming and removing ticks.

Can you find the pouch?

Kangaroos are marsupials — the females have a pouch in which they carry and nurse their young. It is hard to find unless a "joey" (the Australian nick-name for a baby kangaroo) peeks out. New World opossums, koalas, and wallabies are also marsupials.

Try the "kangaroo walk."

The kangaroo pushes its body forward with its hind legs, then puts down its front legs and tail — balancing like a three-legged chair — and swings both hind legs forward. Try it. Would it be easier if you had a tail?

Try the "kangaroo hop."

In "hopping gear," the kangaroo uses only its hind legs to bounce like a rubber ball. Try it. As it hops faster, it holds the tail higher for balance. In "over-drive," the kangaroo makes 40-foot leaps at 40 miles an hour!

48

Kangaroo Air-Conditioning

Kangaroos lick and groom themselves as cats do. There are blood vessels just beneath the skin. When the skin is moistened and then dries, the blood is cooled. The refreshed blood travels to the rest of the body and cools it. Mobs of kangaroos also keep cool on hot days by lying down in the shade and digging a hole in damp, cool earth.

On hot days, kangaroos feed and are more active at night and during the cooler early morning hours.

The Quiet Neighbor

Kangaroos are very quiet. At their loudest, you may hear a grunt or a raspy cough.

Kangaroo Boxing

Kangaroos are generally peaceful animals but they sometimes get angry and fight. They lean back on their tails, box with their front legs, and kick occasionally with their powerful hind legs.

49

Kangaroo Love

• The boomers (males) do a lot of boxing and make low, snorting sounds when the does (females) go into heat.

• The doe is pregnant for 39 days and has one baby.

• The newborn kangaroo is pink, blind, hairless, the size of a lima bean, and weighs one gram!

• Its first trip to the pouch takes three minutes. How does it know where to go since it can't see at birth? By smell? Does the mother lick a trail from birth opening to pouch? Scientists don't know yet.

• The pouch nipple swells in the joey's mouth as he begins to suck the milk. The swollen nipple keeps the baby attached so he won't fall out or get lost.

• Joey stays in the pouch for six months.

• A six-month-old joey weighs six pounds. It has increased its birth weight by 2,700 times in six months. A human baby that weighed six pounds at birth and gained the equivalent weight would weigh 16,000 pounds (two elephants) at six months of age!

• The joey stays with its mother for one year, hopping in and out of the pouch. The pouch expands as he grows.

Veterinarians' Behind the Scenes Info

• To restrain a kangaroo for examination or medical treatment, use the "hugging method." The base of the tail is held while the second person grabs the kangaroo around the chest and holds the front legs.

• In the zoo, kangaroos are fed alfalfa hay, horse and rabbit pellets. In nature, they feed on grasses and browse on low-growing plants.

• Blood samples are taken from the vein on the front leg or on both sides of the tail.

• Sometimes a joey is accidentally evicted from the pouch. Sewing buttons on the pouch (it doesn't hurt the mother) keeps joey from falling out.

• If the joey needs to be hand-raised, a terry cloth towel pouch in an incubator heated to 95° F works well. Joeys can be fed milk replacer formulas (Esbilac) and vitamins with a doll's bottle or a feeding tube.

Kangaroo Stats

Height: 5–7 feet

Weight: 200 lbs.

Heart Rate: 125 beats/minute

Sexually Mature: 2–3 years old

Long Jump: 44 feet

High Jump: 11 feet

Life Span: 10–20 years

Elephants

The elephant is the largest living land animal. It is taller than the ceiling in your home and weighs more than 100 fifth graders all together.

Everyone loves elephants. They make us feel good when we watch how gracefully they move and how loving they are to their babies and to each other. Can you imagine a world without elephants? Unfortunately, every ten minutes, an African elephant is killed. The prize is its tusk, for carving into ivory statues and dagger handles. Elephants' existence on earth may end within our lifetime — unless we all get involved in saving these magnificent creatures.

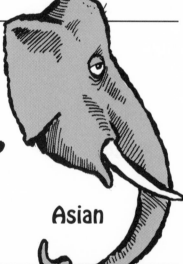

Looking at Elephants

African or Asian?

The African elephant has big, flappy ears and no bumps on the forehead. The Asian has one "finger" on the trunk tip; the African has two.

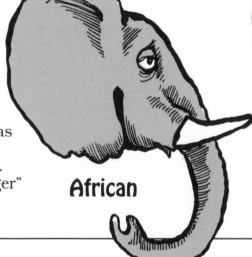

African

Asian

Ears

They are the world's best air conditioners. The ears are loaded with blood vessels. Cool air is brought in contact with blood vessels when the ears are flapped. This cools the blood — and the elephant. Each ear weighs 100 lbs.; that's as much as 10 house cats.

Teeth

They use their tusks (front teeth) to look for food and water. They grow six sets of molars (back teeth) in their lifetime — keeps the "tooth fairy" busy — because the teeth wear out from eating so much rough and coarse food.

Trunk

It is actually a long upper lip and nose combined. Do you breathe through your nose? Elephants breathe mostly (70%) through their trunks. They could use a big hanky when they sneeze. The flexible trunk can pick up small objects like a blade of grass and is used to smell that bag of peanuts in your pocket.

Tail

The few long hairs on the tip are great for chasing away flies. The tail weighs 20 lbs.

Feet

Elephants walk on their toes. Their feet have elastic fatty pads that act as shock absorbers for their massive weight.

Skin

The crease just above the foot is unique to each elephant. It is its "fingerprint." You may notice a white secretion just above the toenails. This is the only spot where the elephant sweats.

If You Invite An Elephant To Dinner...

Here is the zoo diet for one elephant for one year:

• 50,000 lbs. of hay

• 15,000 lbs. of dry alfalfa

• 1,000 lbs. of rolled oats

• 30,000 lbs. of carrots, cabbage, lettuce, and apples

• 16,000 gallons of water. It doesn't have to be expensive, bottled spring water. Thank goodness.

With a diet like this, you may want your elephant-guest to graze outside. In the wild, an elephant spends 18 hours a day eating 600 lbs. of food. You better have a big backyard!

Elephant Language

Listen to the elephants "talk" to each other. They purr, grunt, trumpet, and scream. The trunk will magnify the sounds.

Veterinarians'
Behind the Scenes
Info

• Signs of a sick elephant — will stop constant movement of the trunk, ears, legs, and tail; be less alert and have a decreased appetite.

• How do you take an elephant's temperature? A thermometer is inserted into a fresh bolus (pile) of feces. It sure beats putting a thermometer in their "behind." Normal temp. is about 98° F.

• 100 aspirins three times a day and hosing with cold water will reduce an elephant's fever.

• Elephants are not afraid of mice. And they can forget!

• The elephant's mood changes fast. Keepers must be alert because elephants can be dangerous if they are having a bad moment or a bad day. Being squeezed or trampled by 5 tons is no fun.

Camels

Camels come in two models — the one-humped dromedary and the two-humped bactrian. A simple way to get you "over the hump" of remembering — the dromedary has a "D" on his back and the bactrian has a "B".

The dromedary is found in North Africa, the Middle East, and Australia. (They were imported into Australia.) The bactrian is found in the cold mountain areas of Asia and the Middle Eastern deserts.

Camels are well adapted to desert life. In fact, they have been the main "dune buggy" for 4000 years. They were used in the Middle East for carrying spices from the Far East to Europe in single-file caravans. The bactrian is also at home in the cold mountain areas of Asia where temperatures can plunge to -20° F below zero.

Camels have the same names as horses. The males are called stallions; the females are called mares, and the young camels are foals. Unlike the horse, the camel cannot swim and sinks like a rock.

Looking at Camels

Hump

Dromedaries have one hump; bactrians have two humps. If you jiggle a camel, will you hear water sloshing around in the hump? No. Fat (not water) is stored in the hump. The fat can be converted to energy and water if the camel needs it.

Ears

Tiny earflaps keep sand out of the ear canals.

Eyes

Look at the long eyelashes and large bony eyebrow ridge. Camels also have a third eyelid that slides over the eye like a clear shower curtain. They help protect the camel's eyes from the desert sand and the bright desert sun.

Nostrils

Try closing your nostrils by just thinking about it. Camels can open and close their nostrils. This protects their nose passages when the desert sandstorms start blowing.

Legs

The camel's long legs help it take great strides and carry heavy loads. Its long neck and legs help it see for many miles in the flat desert. The camel lies down like a cow — first folding its front legs under its body, followed by its rear legs and tail end.

Feet

Their big, flat feet prevent the camels from sinking into the sand.

Hot and Cool Camels

Hot camels face the sun, while cool camels turn their side toward the sun. More sunlight will hit the body if it's facing sideways and the camel will warm up.

The Camel's "Bag of Tricks" to Keep from Dying of Thirst

• Don't sweat or pant much.

• Have a pair of kidneys that are very good at saving water for the body.

• Wear a "camel coat" that insulates and keeps the body cool.

• Carry a fatty hump on your back that can be turned into water and energy.

• Have the ability to lose 40 percent of body weight in water (a human would be in trouble if 12 percent of body weight in water were lost).

How do you know when camels are grouchy?

• They spit stomach contents on people, animals, or objects.

• They bite.

• The male sticks out a throat pouch from his mouth and makes loud, threatening noises.

Camel Dining

In nature: graze on herbs, grasses, and thin branches.

In the zoo: timothy or alfalfa hay is fed in convenient eye-level hay racks.

This is supplemented with vitamins, minerals, salt blocks, and a commercial dairy (cow) concentrate.

The inner camel — Where does the food go?

Into a stomach with three compartments. The camel does not have a gallbladder.

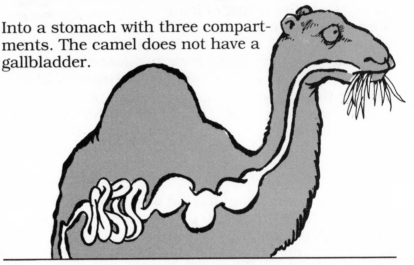

Camel Stats:

Sexually Mature at: 2–2 1/2 years of age

Gestation (Pregnancy): 350–390 days (usually one foal)

Birth Weight: 75–100 lbs.

Average Adult Weight: 1200 lbs.

Life Span: 20 years

Strength: can carry 1000 lbs. on their back (6 average-size men)

Giraffes

Giraffes are the tallest of land animals. Their necks can be six feet long — almost one-third of their length. That would be like a six-foot person having a two-foot neck. Imagine if you had a two-foot-long neck. How would it change the way you do simple things like walk, sleep, eat, or pick up an object on the floor? An interesting fact — giraffes have seven neck bones — the same number that you do, but each one is ten inches long.

Giraffes do everything in a big way. Their two-foot-long heart pumps 20 gallons of blood every minute. In the zoo, they will eat about 50 lbs. of food a day and will wash it down with 20 gallons of water.

Giraffes live on the plains of Africa and love to eat the leaves of trees.

Looking at Giraffes

Head

A giraffe's head is two feet long. The head and neck together weigh 500 lbs.

Neck

The spots on the neck have a unique pattern for each giraffe — its "fingerprints." The neck vein (jugular) has a valve to regulate blood flow when the long neck is up in the air or down to the ground. Otherwise, giraffes would have "fainting spells" from lack of blood and oxygen to the brain.

Horns

Females and young males have hair on their horn tips. Mature males don't because they fight with their horns and rub off the hair. Males also have longer horns.

Tongue

The giraffe's tongue is 20 inches long — as long as two or three of your feet lined end to end. It is a great tool for stripping acacia leaves off branches.

Tail

The thick hairs on the tip of the tail keep flies and other insects away.

Jogging Like a Giraffe

An average human adult has a two-foot stride. An average giraffe has a 15-foot stride. Its gallop can hit speeds of 35 m.p.h. The fastest human can reach a speed of 25 m.p.h., thoroughbred horses 40 m.p.h.

Veterinarians' Behind the Scenes Info

• In the zoo, a giraffe likes to munch on 20 lbs. of alfalfa hay and 10 lbs. of horse chow every day, as well as carrots, rolled oats, apples, potato, cabbage, bread, banana, and other greens, vegetables, and fruits. Can you find hay racks in the feeding area? They are placed at eye level because giraffes are high browsers.

• With what tool does the veterinarian commonly examine a giraffe? Binoculars. Restraining a giraffe can be very stressful and dangerous to the animal and the zoo staff, so observing a sore or other signs of illness from a distance can often be very helpful. Medications can be mixed in the food.

Giraffe Stats

Height: 14 to 16 feet
6 feet (at birth)

Weight: 1100 to 1700 lbs. (adult)
150 lbs. (at birth)

Sexually Mature:
3 1/2 years of age

Gestation (Pregnancy): 14 months; usually has one baby

Life Span: 25 years

Hippopotamuses

The hippopotamus was called the "Libyan monster" in ancient times by early Greek explorers in Africa. In later journeys, this huge, strange creature was named the "river horse" — Hippo (horse), potamus (river). The Romans were the first to discover that the pig — not the horse — was a distant relative of the hippo. The swine and the hippo have a simple digestive system and an even number of toes.

Today, hippos are only found along the riverbanks and reedy shores of Africa. Long ago, they flourished in all parts of the Old World — even in what is now England.

The hippo is found in folktales and religion. Epet, the hippopotamus goddess of ancient Egypt, guided souls during their hazardous journey to the underworld. In ancient Rome, gladiator combat wasn't the only popular sport. Hippos were pitted against lions and crocodiles in the coliseums.

Looking at the Hippopotamus

Head

The head may be all that you can see of the partially submerged hippo. The hippo's head may be 25 percent of its weight — half a ton (1,000 lbs.), and may be 3 1/2 feet long.

Ears and Nostrils

When the hippo goes underwater, its small ears fold over and slitlike nostrils form a watertight shield. Watch how a wiggle of the ears and a loud snort removes water when the hippo surfaces.

Mouth

A dentist's dream! Open wide. A four-foot gap separates the upper and lower teeth in a full yawn. When the hippo is underwater with its mouth closed, the upper lip forms a watertight seal.

Teeth

Only half of the razor-sharp canine teeth are exposed. They are over three feet long and each weighs seven pounds. They could bite a human in half! The back teeth (molars) are flat for chewing vegetation. If they wear down, the hippo cannot chew and dies of starvation.

64

Skin

The hippo's skin is two inches thick and, although it looks hairless, the hippo has very short hairs over its body. Glands in the skin exude a thick, red, oily substance which protects the hippo from prolonged water or sun exposure. It is not "sweating blood!"

Legs

The hippo's legs are short and stubby and are made to hold its weight of two tons. The toes are covered with a black hoof.

Speaking "Hippo"

- **"I'm angry"** — Deep roars, growls, and bellows.

- **"I'm excited"** — Neigh like a horse.

- **"I'm looking for a mate"** — Romantically moo.

- **Fighting** — Squeal like a pig.

- **"Just clearing my nose"** — Snort.

Hippos are generally peaceful creatures, but when they get angry, they usually opt for threat displays. They open their mouths wide, yawn, bellow, and bellyflop in the water. The other hippo will show submission by lowering its head.

Territory · Eating · Breathing

"This is My Property, Keep Out"

Humans might put up a distinctive fence, mailbox, or sign to mark territory. Male hippos scatter their feces with their tail to say, "This is my property."

Salad . . . Please.

• In nature, 40 lbs. of grasses, leaves, and aquatic plants are eaten.

• In the zoo, hay, grains, potatoes, carrots, apples, and bread are served.

Try Holding Your Breath Like a Hippo

They can stay underwater for 4–5 minutes. Time it.

Veterinarians' Behind the Scenes Info

- Hippos don't need vaccinations.

- Hippos are so powerful, they could destroy a truck. They are put in a crate when moved.

- If medication is needed, it may be mixed in vegetables or mixed with molasses before being put in the grain. If injections of medicine or anesthesia are required, dart guns or pole syringes are used.

Hippo Stats

Height:
4 1/2 feet (Nile hippo)

Length:
11 1/2 feet (Nile hippo)

Weight:
500 lbs. (Pygmy hippo)
4,000 lbs. (2 tons)
(Nile hippo)

Heart Rate:
50–80 beats
per minute

Breathing Rate:
12 breaths per minute

Sexually Mature:
2 years old (Pygmy)
7 years old (Nile)

Gestation (Pregnancy):
200 days (Pygmy)
240 days (Nile)

Birth Weight:
15 lbs. (Pygmy)
90 lbs. (Nile)

Baby's Length:
3 feet (Nile)

Baby's Height:
15" tall (Nile)

Rhinoceroses

Next to the elephant, the rhinoceros is the second largest land mammal. Rhinoceroses have thick legs and compact, massive bodies.

Rhinoceros means "horned nose" (ancient Greek). They are the only animal on earth with horns on their nose. The horn grows continuously and will be completely replaced in one or two years if knocked off. It would probably be a great place to position a pair of glasses, since the rhino is extremely nearsighted and can't see faraway objects very well.

Who's Who?

	Horns	Upper Lip	"Armor" Skin Plates
Black (African)	2	Hooked	No
White (African)	2	Square	No
Indian (Asian)	1	Hooked	Yes
Javan (Asian)	1	Hooked	Yes
Sumatran (Asian)	2	Hooked	No

BLACK

INDIAN

SUMATRAN

JAVAN

WHITE

Looking At Rhinoceroses

Head

What does a headache feel like in a 2,000 lb. head? Ask a white rhino. It needs a lot of muscles to hold up such a heavy head. That hump on the white rhino is the great muscle holding up that beautiful head.

Horns

Their horns are made of keratin, like your fingernails. They also grow continuously. The longest horn ever measured was 5 1/2 feet long and belonged to a white rhino.

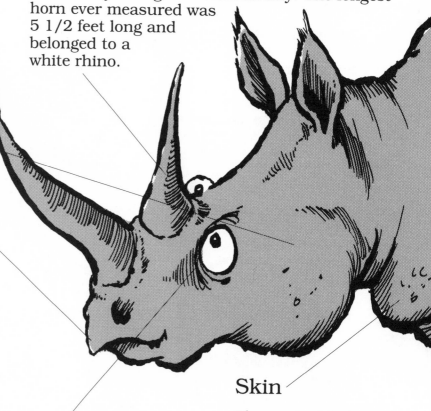

Lip

You will know what rhinos eat in nature by looking at the shape of the upper lip. "Square Lip" is a lawnmower — grass grazer. "Hook Lip" is a browser of bushes and trees.

Eyes

Chances are that, if you are 15 feet or more away from the rhino, it won't be able to see you very well (especially the black rhino), They are nearsighted and can't see objects that are far away. Their wonderful sense of hearing and smell make up for their poor eyesight.

Skin

The neck skin is one inch thick! The Indian rhino's skin of platelike folds is even thicker. Rhino skin does not have a good blood supply, so skin wounds heal very slowly.

Body and Legs

If rhinos were football players, they would be the world's greatest fullbacks. They are all muscle and thick bones — a powerful combination that can propel their 4,000 lbs. at 35 miles per hour. A charging rhino can easily turn over a small truck. It's surprising that there are no football teams with the nickname or mascot "Rhinos."

The White Rhino

The white rhino is actually gray. Its name comes from the Afrikanner word "wyd," referring to its *wide*, square lip.

Feet

A three-toed hoof with a cushion pad behind the toes helps support the tremendous weight.

How To Keep That "Dirty Look"

Rhinos love to take mud and dust baths. This cools them and keeps away biting insects.

Personality Plus — Rhino-Style

The white rhino is a social animal that likes to live in herds. The black rhino likes to be by itself and is more grouchy. It may even charge a train if it's having a bad day.

Rhino Cuisine in the Zoo

The rhinoceros eats about 100 lbs. of hay, grains, fruit, and yellow vegetables every day.

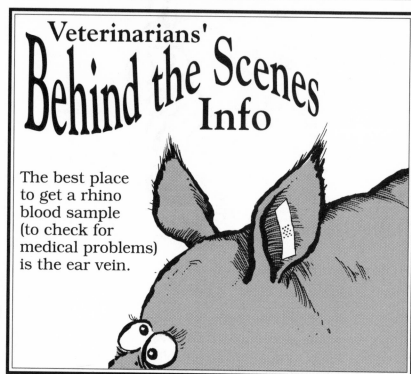

Veterinarians' Behind the Scenes Info

The best place to get a rhino blood sample (to check for medical problems) is the ear vein.

Rhinoceros Stats

Weight:
3000 to 5,500 lbs.

Length:
14 to 16 feet long

Heart Rate:
65 beats per minute

Sexual Maturity:
4 1/2 years of age

Gestation (Pregnancy):
15 months (450 days)

Newborn Rhinos:
80 lbs. and 1 1/2 ft. tall
(a big baby)

Running Speed:
35 miles per hour

Swimming: like a duck. Asian rhinos are excellent swimmers.

Zebras

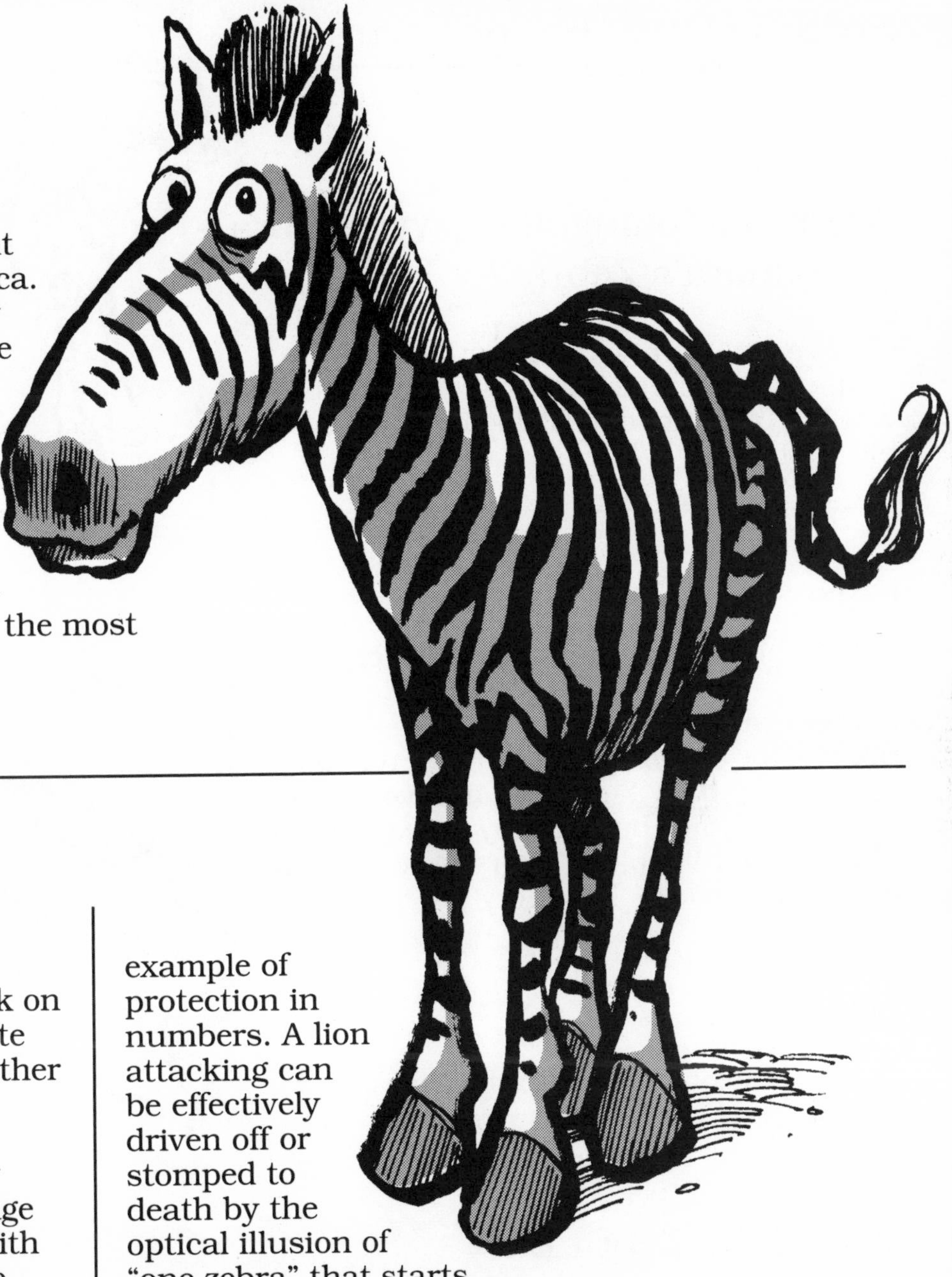

Zebras are abundant
on the plains of Africa.
In fact, it is the only
place on earth where
the expression
"when you hear
hoofbeats, don't
look for zebras"
(instead, look for
horses) would not
be true. The expres-
sion means look for the most
logical answer.

Looking at Zebras

Stripes

Are the stripes black on
a white body or white
on a black body? Either
answer is correct.

The stripes are very
important camouflage
— for blending in with
tall grass. When the
zebras are in a group, it
is difficult to tell where
one zebra begins and
the other ends. The
zebra is a perfect
example of
protection in
numbers. A lion
attacking can
be effectively
driven off or
stomped to
death by the
optical illusion of
"one zebra" that starts
kicking with 20 hooves (5 zebras).

Each zebra has its own stripe pattern — its "fingerprints" — on its shoulders and hindquarters. Can
you see the difference in each zebra?

Are You Looking at Grevy's Zebra or Damara's Zebra ?

Grevy's has narrow black and white stripes. Damara's has widely spaced stripes with a brown shadow stripe between the black stripes.

Ears

Zebras hear danger approaching very well.

Human ears are useless for showing emotion. We rely on facial expression, body language, and voice. But you can tell how a zebra feels by its ears; ears straight up ("I'm okay"), ears forward (fear), ears pulled back ("I'm angry").

Lips

The soft, flexible lips help the zebra gather food.

Watch the Zebra Eat

For the "workhorse" teeth — the front teeth (incisors) bite off the food. The flat, sharp basic teeth (molars) crush and grind the food. In nature, zebras dine on vegetation. In the zoo, timothy hay (20 lbs. daily), grass, carrots, corn, and vitamins keep zebras happy. A salt block is provided at all times.

Watch the Zebras Groom

Zebras love to roll on the ground and rub against trees, boulders, and even other zebras. The dust and mud collected in rolling helps protect their skin from insects and the drying effect of the sun and hot winds. They love neck and shoulder nibbles, and massages from other zebras. In nature, the tick bird "rides the zebra" and eats the pesky insects.

"Speaking" Like a Zebra

The plains zebra barks like a dog. He has different sounds for greeting, alarm, pain, and "I'm okay."

Zebra Stats

Height (at shoulder): 60 inches (5 feet)

Weight: 500–600 lbs.

Body Temp.: 101° F (same as the dog and cat)

Heart Rate: 70 beats/minute

Gestation (Pregnancy): 11–13 months

Offspring: 1

Speed: 60 miles per hour (short distances), 35 miles per hour (longer distances)

Life Span: 25 years

Bears

Bears are one of the most loved animals in the zoo. They are very popular in fairy tales and fiction where they are given human qualities. They are natural clowns and look cuddly — but they have great strength in their compact bodies and can be dangerous when they are adults. In nature, bears like to be by themselves. They socialize only during the breeding season. The male is called a boar and the female, a sow.

Looking at Bears

Paws and Claws

The bear's claws are longer on the front feet than the back feet. They are used for digging, opening up beehives, climbing trees, catching fish, and for protection. The claws are as long as a child's hand!

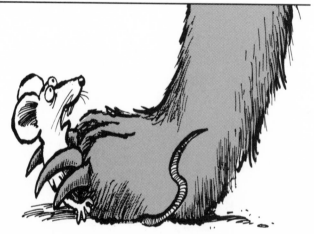

Footpads

Pads made of hard skin cover the bottom of the feet and protect and cushion them. If wild bears hibernate too long because the weather remains cold, they may get a "tender foot" problem. The pads will become sore and raw from lack of vitamins. It can be treated by feeding the bear a well-balanced diet supplemented by extra B vitamins.

Teeth

The long canine teeth are used for catching and killing prey and tearing food. The cheek teeth (molars) grind the meat or plant food.

Look at the Bear's Body

Underneath the thick hair coat and skin is a huge fat layer for insulation and as a food reserve. The fat layer is thickest over the rump and thigh.

Watch the Bear Walk

Bears are "pigeon-toed" — their front feet turn in. When they walk, their front and back legs on the same side move forward together. Is this different from the elephant? Giraffe? Dogs? Cats? Try walking like these animals. When you are riding in your car, see how fast 35 miles per hour feels. Some bears can run that fast for short distances.

"Bearly" Awake

The "winter sleep" is not a true hibernation because bears can be easily awakened, and they move around during warm weather. Their heart rate during the winter sleep is 20–30 beats per minute.

Veterinarians'
Behind the Scenes
Info

• An upset stomach is a common bear medical problem. When it comes to eating, bears are "pigs." They'll even eat dirt or sand.

• Upset stomachs are treated by not giving food for a day, ice cubes to lick, Kaopectate, and, if their stomach feels better the next day, baby food to eat.

• The zoo diet consists of dog food-based diets, fruits, vegetables, or a commercial bear diet.

• Although injections can be given, it is much easier to put the medicine in sweet foods such as fruits.

• The neck and shoulder areas are the best for injections. These areas have the least fat.

• Needles have to be longer than three inches so that they can reach the muscle layer.

• A squeeze cage, pole or projectile syringe may be used to administer the medication or sedative.

• The dentist is one of the bear's best friends. Bears frequently crack or break a tooth. Root canals and silver fillings make the situation "bear-able."

• Since bears don't brush after every meal, tartar buildup can be a problem. Regular dental cleaning (under anesthesia, of course) is helpful in keeping the teeth and gums healthy.

• Metal plates are surgically placed on a bear's broken bone for good healing because a bear will chew or claw off a cast.

Bear Stats

Height:
4-5 feet Malayan sun bear, Spectacled, Sloth, and Asiatic black bear

8-9 feet Polar and Great Brown bear

Body Temp.:
99.6° F–101° F

Breathing and Heart Rates:
Same as humans

Weight:
60–130 lbs. Malayan

200 lbs. Sloth, Spectacled, Asiatic Black bear

800–1500 lbs. Great Brown and Polar bears

Polar Bears

"Let's go out for seafood."

In the wild, the polar bear spends most of its waking hours shopping for food. It may walk several miles to find its seal or fish dinner. Polar bears are very patient creatures because seals are not cooperative dinner guests. They are hard to catch — most get away.

Polar bears are found at the top of the world — the Arctic Circle. There are only an estimated 15,000 polar bears in existence. An international agreement has been signed to protect the polar bear. Not only must large wilderness areas be set aside to ensure the survival of the polar bear, but we must make sure that oil drilling and new towns do not upset the delicate balance of nature. Fish need clean water and plenty of plant life. Fish are eaten by seals and polar bears eat the seals.

Looking at Polar Bears

Ears

They are very small. If the ear flaps were larger, they would freeze and too much body heat would be lost through them.

Head

A long nose helps a polar bear smell a seal more than three miles away. That's a real "seal of approval!"

Fur Coat

The sunlight bounces off the *hollow* hairs and only *looks* white. The warm sun rays are absorbed by the polar bear's *black* skin. The haircoat has air pockets like a down jacket which trap warm air.

Paws

Sharp claws and 25 lb., 1 1/2 foot long, 1 foot wide paws swiftly ensure that a fish or seal meal stays for dinner. The paws and claws are also used by males during the mating season — when they fight over a female.

Look at the thick, rough footpads. They protect the paws from freezing or slipping on the ice — polar bear four-wheel drive.

Shape

The polar bear is a blubber ball. A four-inch fat layer protects it from the icy cold water. The fat layer, thick bones, and enormous muscles contribute to its great shape.

Seal Is Not on the Zoo Menu

In the zoo, a commercial chow or a high protein dog chow mixed with some vegetables, bread, meat and fish products is the "Catch of the Day."

The Polar Bear's Reputation

Polar bears are considered the most dangerous animals in most zoos. "Glad to meet you" and "glad to eat you" mean the same thing to the polar bear.

Mothering, Polar-Bear Style

• They are very loving, caring mothers.

• In nature, one or two cubs weighing about one pound each are born and nursed in a den (with a long entrance tunnel) under the ice and snow.

• In the zoo, a den with piles of straw is provided. It is isolated from the other bears and is kept quiet and has soft light.

• In the zoo, many bear cubs have been hand-raised from birth. They are fed a formula containing puppy milk replacer (Esbilac), whipping cream, water, and multi-vitamins. They are placed in a warm incubator and given much love and attention.

• The cubs leave the den when they are three months old and weigh about 20 lbs.

Polar Bear Stats

Height: 10 1/2 feet

Weight: 700–1,400 lbs.

Body Temp.: 100° F.

Heart Rate:
70 beats per minute
(What's yours?)

Breathing Rate:
15–30 breaths per minute (Count a bear's breathing rate)

Wild Diet:
seals and fish

Gestation (Pregnancy):
6–9 months
(1–2 cubs born)

Birth Weight:
1 lb. (less than most humans)

Life Span:
40+ years

Cats

Cats have been around for more than 50 million years, since the saber-tooth tiger roamed the earth.

Except for the North and South Poles and a few islands, cats are found all over the world. They have survived for millions of years because they have adapted to all sorts of places; hot jungles, tropical rainforests, deserts, mountains, swamps, and open grasslands.

In nature, cats are meat eaters (carnivores), but they also eat the bones and stomach contents of their prey — for a balanced diet. We eat a balanced diet also. We don't just eat meat, for example, we include milk products and vegetables.

Lions, tigers, leopards, and jaguars are members of the "big cat" group. Your house cat may think he is a big cat at times, but there are major differences besides size. When looking at the cats in the zoo, study their behavior. Are they big cats or little cats?

Big Cats

- They roar.

- Purr only when breathing out (exhaling).

- Are not enthusiastic groomers. They rub or lick their forepaws, nose, and groin.

- Eat lying down.

- Rest with their front paws out in front and tail straight back.

Little Cats

- They have a high-pitched scream.

- Can purr continuously while breathing in and out.

- Like to spend a lot of time grooming. They lick the fur all over their bodies.

- Eat in a crouched position.

- Like to rest with their front paws curled under their body.

Looking at Cats

Eyes

The cat's eyes are on the side of the head so it can see in many directions.

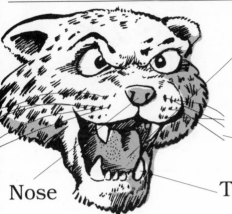

Tongue

The tongue has barbs for scraping meat off the bones. It is also a wonderful grooming tool. The little cats love to keep themselves clean.

Nose

Cats have outstanding noses. They can smell animals and humans who crossed their trail hours before.

Teeth

The long, sharp canine teeth grab and hold the prey. The molar or back teeth are the "meat grinders."

Whiskers

The whiskers help the cat "feel" in the dark.

Feet

Cats walk on their toes. The heels of their feet are off the ground. Can you find the heel? The sharp claws can be retracted (pulled back). Soft pads, claw retraction, and walking on tiptoes allow cats to walk quietly, stalk their prey, and leap on it from a short distance.

Bodies

All cats are very muscular. They are also very flexible, graceful, and agile creatures.

85

Fur

The color and pattern of the fur is "purr-fect" camouflage. By their fur, find the cats that live on the African plains . . . tropical jungles . . . snowy Siberia. For example, what color would the snow leopard be for camouflage?

Veterinarians' Behind the Scenes Info

• Wild cats are very territorial. If a new cat is being introduced in the zoo, it is kept within sight and smell range so the other cats can get to know it. Sometimes moving the cats to an area where none has "territorial rights" helps.

• Lions do well in a group (called a pride of lions), while other cats are more solitary by nature.

• Wild cats receive the same vaccinations as your house cat.

• Cats need their teeth cleaned regularly — under anesthesia, of course.

Cats n' Stats

Body Temperature:	Heart Rate (large cats):	Breathing Rate:
100–102° F	40–50 per minute	10–30 per minute
	(small cats):	
	80–125 per minute	Bones in the Body:
		230 +

Wolves

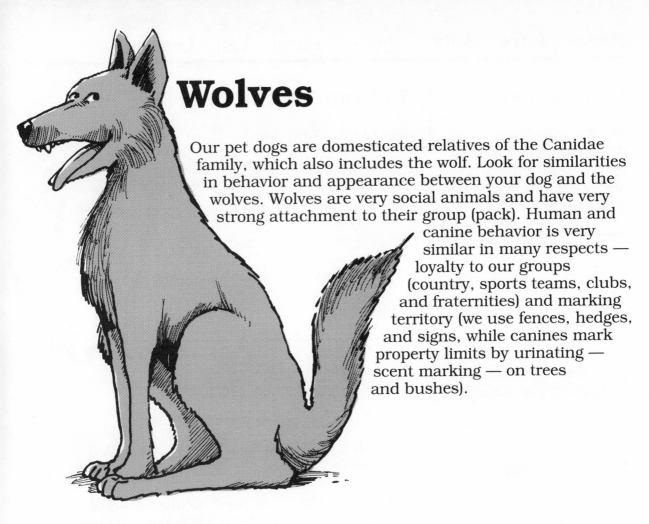

Our pet dogs are domesticated relatives of the Canidae family, which also includes the wolf. Look for similarities in behavior and appearance between your dog and the wolves. Wolves are very social animals and have very strong attachment to their group (pack). Human and canine behavior is very similar in many respects — loyalty to our groups (country, sports teams, clubs, and fraternities) and marking territory (we use fences, hedges, and signs, while canines mark property limits by urinating — scent marking — on trees and bushes).

Looking at Wolves

Fangs

The long, sharp fangs (canine teeth) are used for grabbing the prey and holding on until it is brought down. The wolves' fangs are longer than ours because we never had to hunt prey in the same way.

Ears

Watch the wolves rotate their ears and point them in the direction of sounds. They are able to hear another howling wolf pack several miles away.

The Wolf Walk

Wolves (like dogs, cats, and horses) walk on their "fingertips" and "tiptoes." For example, the "heel" of the wolf's rear leg sticks up in the air.

Can you see it?

The long legs help them run faster by lengthening their stride and giving them a powerful kick.

Wolf Playtime

• Bowing low with front legs and wagging the tail vigorously means "let's play!" (just like your dog's play signal). What signals do you give your friends when you want to play?

• Leaping in a zigzag fashion also means let's play "chase, tumble, and wrestle."

"Tail Talk" — The Tale of the Tail

Held high — intimidate

Straight out — attack

Up and wagging — playful

Hanging down — relaxed

Slightly under the body — humble

Hidden under body — fearful

Can you find the "top dog" in the pack?

The male and female wolf leaders are called the "alphas."

• When meeting other pack members, alphas hold their ears up and tail high while bottom dogs' ears are down and the tail is tucked between their legs.

Smell Sense and Territory Scents

• Wolves can smell you a mile away.

• In nature, an alpha (leader) makes a scent mark (urinates on an object, for example) or inspects a scent mark, on the average, every two minutes.

Cool Wolves

• Panting.

• Sweating from the paw bottoms.

• Finding a shady spot.

• Digging a hole.

Aw, Mom, Mice and Rabbit Again For Dinner? Let's Go Out For Moose.

• In nature, wild mice, rabbits, birds, fish, and crabs are the common prey.

• Moose are not an easy dinner. A full-grown male moose weighing 1300 lbs. attacks with its antlers and heavy hooves.

• Most moose (90 percent) outrun or outfight a pack of wolves.

Meet the Wolf Family

• The pack is loving and caring to the pups.

• In nature, in most packs, the alpha male and female mate and reproduce only with each other. This ensures survival of the strongest.

• The mother gives birth in a den (a hollow log, a rock cave, or an old beaver house or a burrow).

• The other pack members are like uncles, aunts, and cousins — feeding (regurgitating food for the pups), playing, and pup-sitting for the little ones.

Veterinarians' Behind the Scenes Info

• The wolf is easy to tame if socialized to humans at 6–8 weeks of age, just like dogs.

• Zoo wolves eat dry or canned dog food.

Wolf Stats

Height: 3 feet

Length: 6 feet

Weight: 80-100 lbs.

Body Temp.:
101° F

Heart Rate:
85 beats per minute

Breathing Rate:
12 breaths per minute

Gestation (Pregnancy):
63 days

Litter Size: 3-13 pups

Birth Weight: 1 lb.

Eyes Open:
10-14 days

Running Speed:
35 miles per hour

Life Span:
14-16 years

Primates

When we look at primates, we are looking at ourselves.

Primates (and humans) . . .
- have hair rather than feathers or scales.
- have flat faces.
- use facial expressions to show emotions.
- can sit or stand on their hind legs.
- manipulate things with their hands.
- have fingernails and fingerprints.
- babies are nursed.
- babies are nurtured and protected by their immediate and extended families.

The larger "great" apes are the gorillas, chimpanzees, and orangutans. The smaller "lesser" apes include monkeys and two groups of tree-dwelling acrobats that can leap more than 30 feet from branch to branch: the gibbons and siamangs.

Monkeys

"He's making a monkey out of him," "Don't monkey around," "He's having as much fun as a barrel full of monkeys," "Monkey see, monkey do." Do you see similarities between our behavior and that of monkeys? Monkeys are one of the most popular animals to watch because they are so human-like (or are we monkeylike?).

Monkeys are divided into Old World and New World groups. Old World monkeys have prehensile tails that can be used for swinging, holding, or grabbing onto an object (like a fifth "hand"). Most New World monkeys do not have prehensile tails. Old Worlds have 32 teeth; New Worlds have 36 teeth. While at the zoo, see if you can "tell from the tail" if they are Old or New World because they are not going to say "Ahhhh" so that you can count their teeth. The Old Worlds include the baboons, mandrills, and macaques. The New Worlds include the squirrel, spider, woolly, capuchin, marmoset, and howler monkeys. The Golden Tamarin, a very endangered species, is also a New World monkey.

Monkeys are found in the tropical and semitropical areas of Africa, Asia, Central and South America. They like to "monkey around" in a group called a troop.

Looking at Monkeys

Playing

The rough-and-tumble play of monkeys and young children is very much alike. Watch them run, chase, flee, wrestle, jump up and down with both feet together, laugh, and fall onto a soft surface — "monkey tag."

Facial Expressions and Body Posture

You be the scientist. What do you think monkeys are communicating when they make a certain face and stand a certain way? For example, look for the "play face" seen during playful wrestling and tumbling. The mouth is open wide, but the lips cover the teeth — a nonthreatening gesture. Do you think that monkeys and other animals have the same feelings as you do — happiness, sadness, fear?

Sounds

Listen to the sounds that a monkey makes. What is it trying to say?

Smells

Humans have very weak noses, so we find it difficult to study the odor signals of monkeys and other animals. Odor signals are very important in animal communication.

Eating Habits

Watch the monkeys eat. Do they have a favorite food? Some of the Old World monkeys cram their mouths with food, storing it in cheek pouches. Then they scamper off to a safe place to dine at their leisure. Do you see any monkeys with bulging faces?

Grooming

Monkeys love to groom each other. Grooming removes dead skin and parasites but, more important, it strengthens their friendships. Watch how one hand parts the hair and the other hand searches the skin area. The monkey being groomed appears relaxed — almost in a trance.

Veterinarians' Behind the Scenes Info

• A new monkey must be formally introduced to a troop. A barrier separates the monkey so that they can smell, hear, see, and touch each other. When they start grooming each other, the barrier can safely come down.

• Monkeys need a balanced diet just like humans — meats, grains, fruits, and vegetables. People should not feed monkeys only bananas.

• Older monkeys are prone to strokes just like older humans and parrots.

• Owl monkeys have a natural anti-clotting substance in their blood-stream that is six times higher than humans, so they tend to bleed longer if they get a cut.

Monkey Stats

Body Temperature: 101.8° F

Heart Rate: 100–200 beats per minute

Sexual Maturity: 2–4 years of age

Gestation (Pregnancy): 140–170 days

Gorillas

There are three types of gorillas in Africa — the Western and Lowland from the tropical forests of West Africa; Eastern Lowland from the central African rainforests; and the Mountain gorillas from evergreen slopes 8,000 feet high.

Looking at Gorillas

Head Shape and Color

The lowland gorilla has a rounded head with short, orange-brown hair. The mountain gorilla's head is high-domed.

Ears

Gorillas have small ears, probably because they don't socialize by long-distance hooting in chorus, as do the big-eared chimps.

Mouth

The enormous gorilla is a plant eater. Among primates, only humans are killers and meat eaters on a large scale.

Arms

The arms are about one foot longer than an adult human's and much more muscular. In fact, an adult male gorilla could lift five lions!

Hands

Like humans, gorillas have five sturdy, tough fingers, fingernails, and finger-prints. The thumb is shorter but is still used to grab things. The palm is very wide. 90 percent of gorillas are right-handed. How about the gorillas that you are watching?

Belly

A human with a "beer belly" would be considered out of shape. Gorillas need the large belly to house all the bulky food that they eat.

Facial Expressions

We know that gorillas and other animals have feelings. For example, Koko is a female gorilla that lives in the San Francisco Zoo. She learned sign language. On her twelfth birthday she signed that she would like a cat for a present. She chose a tailless (Manx) kitten that she named "All Ball." Koko loved All Ball and gently carried her. Koko was very sad when All Ball was hit by a car and died. Gorillas feel sadness just as you and I do. Although Koko will always have a special place in her heart for All Ball, she adopted another kitten to love and signed her name — Lipstick. Is the gorilla that you are watching happy, sad, angry, fearful, curious, excited? Gorillas even shed tears.

Walking

Adult gorillas spend most of their time on the ground where they prefer to walk on all fours. The gorilla "knuckle-walks" on its fingers and has a thickened "walking pad" on the top of each finger. Try walking like a gorilla. Is it comfortable?

Gorilla Fun

• Eating (30–40 lbs. of food per day).

• Napping.

• Foraging (looking for food); in nature, gorillas have a 10–15 mile range in which they find their plants, stems, vines, leaves, and fruit.

• Grooming — the females like to groom their infants and each other.

• Sunbathing.

• Playing — young children and young gorillas are alike in many ways — climbing, playing "king of the mountain," wrestling, and chasing each other. They are very active.

The Gorilla Family

• Gorillas are wonderful parents.

• In nature, 5–30 gorillas move in a group called a *troop*.

• An older male, a *silverback*, is usually the family head. He has gray hair on his back.

• Gorilla mothers learn how to care for their babies by watching other mothers.

• In nature, the young gorilla stays with its mother for three years.

Family and Neighborly Arguments

• Gorillas are very peaceful, gentle, and shy but like all of us, do get angry at times.

• When gorillas have a mild argument, they may stare angrily and push each other.

• An angry male roars or beats his chest and even charges. Most gorilla charges end before contact — the "Gorilla Bluff."

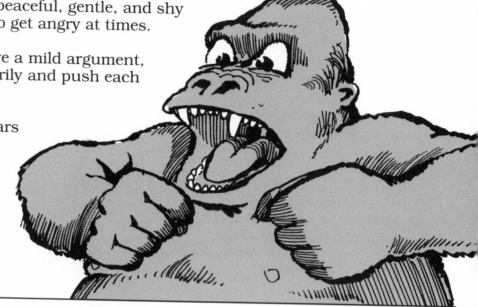

Gorilla Stats

Height: 5–6 feet

Weight:
175 lbs. (females),
350 lbs. (males)

Arm Length:
4 feet long
(human, 3 feet long)

Leg Length: 3 feet long

Body Temp.:
98.6° F
(same as humans)

Heart Rate:
100 beats per minute

Breathing Rate:
12 breaths per minute

Sexually Mature:
6–7 years old

Gestation (Pregnancy):
251–295 days

Chimpanzees

The chimp is the noisiest and most active of the Great Apes. It thumps its feet and bangs on trees in the forest to keep in touch with group members — a primate telephone system. It screams, shouts, or barks as its mood changes.

Chimpanzees are very social and move in groups of 20–40 through the tropical forests of Africa. There are three different chimpanzee populations — Eastern, Western, and Pygmy.

Chimps make us laugh. Is it because the chimps act so much like humans? Scientists generally agree that chimpanzees and other apes differ only by degree from humans — they feel, think, can communicate with sign language, make tools ("leaf sponges," "leaf chopsticks," to pull termites from holes), and, as we are just discovering, have a social organization similar to our own.

Looking at Chimpanzees

Watch the Chimp Move

Does the chimp move like the gorilla? Yes and no. Gorillas and chimps prefer to "knuckle-walk" using all four limbs. Chimps like to leap and (although not as much as gibbons) they *brachiate* — swing along and between branches from the hands, with the body hanging free.

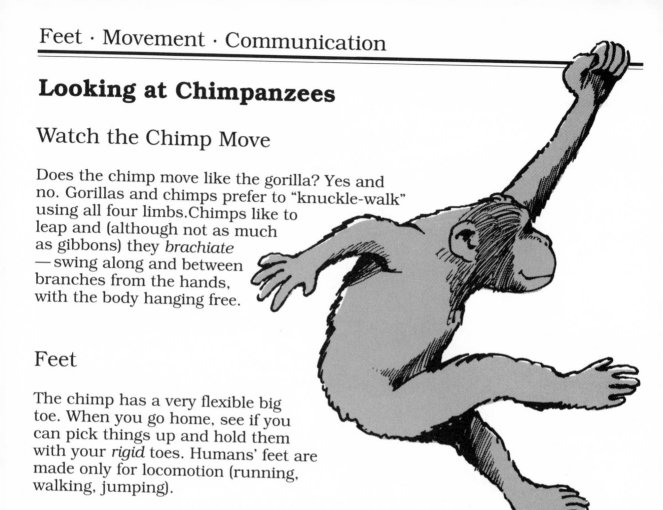

Feet

The chimp has a very flexible big toe. When you go home, see if you can pick things up and hold them with your *rigid* toes. Humans' feet are made only for locomotion (running, walking, jumping).

Watch the Chimp Communicate

After watching the chimps, you will discover that they seem so human — or do we seem so chimplike? Here is a short course in chimp language:

• Bare the teeth means "I'm upset."

• Screaming or yelping with a "fear" face means "I'm scared."

• Fewer teeth showing is a "play" face. Commonly seen during wrestling and tickling games.

• Panting sounds are the "chimp laugh."

• Holding out a hand means begging for food or for support during an argument. If two chimps are arguing, a hand may be held out to a third chimp to "side with him." Do humans sometimes do this?

• Hug and kiss — affection or making up after an argument.

Pretend . . .

that you are the first human to observe the chimp. What kind of behavior, friendships, and feelings do you see? Is any of it similar to human behavior? Take notes. Draw pictures. Do the females like to sit in a group and self-groom? Do teenage girls like to do the same thing? Which males act aggressively by making their hair stand on end? Which chimp is the leader? Which are having a conflict? Who is the peacemaker?

Watch the Chimps Eat

In nature, they forage and feed on fruits, leaves, flowers, and insects. In the zoo, some food (sunflower seeds) is hidden by keepers to allow the chimps to forage. They are also fed monkey pellets, dog food, fruits, vegetables, and rabbit pellets. Which chimps are neat eaters? Which are messy? Are the most aggressive chimps also the messiest?

Meet the Chimp Family

• Adults are very loving to baby chimps. Watch them.

• At birth, the newborn chimp is weak and helpless and weighs 3 lbs.

• A baby chimp is breast-fed every hour.

• The baby chimp hangs on its mother's belly hair as she moves around.

• The baby's white tail tuft disappears at 6 months of age.

• 6 months is the beginning of chimp "toddlerhood." The mother now teaches her little one the rules of chimp etiquette since group members grow intolerant if the chimp "goes ape."

• The young chimp stays with its mother for four years.

Learning to be Friends

Watch the young chimps wrestle, tickle, and groom each other. This play helps them become friends.

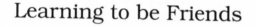

Orangutans

Oran-outang means "old man of the forest" in the Borneo language. Orangutans existed in the early Stone Age 35,000 years ago. They were on the caveman's menu.

Today, orangutans live only in remote jungles on the islands of Borneo and Sumatra. Probably only a few thousand remain because their habitat is being destroyed. It is important that we humans make sure that orangutans do not disappear from our earth and, in fact, that we help them flourish.

Orangutans are considered one of the most intelligent animals on earth.

Looking at Orangutans

Is he from Borneo or Sumatra?

A male orangutan from Sumatra has an elongated face, long mustache and beard. His male Bornean relative will have pebbly-skinned cheek flaps that get larger with age and no long flowing beard or mustache. Can you find Borneo and Sumatra on a map?

Arms and Hands

The orangutan's arms are very long and can hook around vines and limbs — well suited for a "swinging" life in high trees.

Notice that the thumb is shorter and lacks the grasping ability of humans.

They have fingerprints like humans.

Feet

The orangutan's feet are for grabbing tree branches. Human toes are shorter and the big toe is not placed properly for gripping a tree branch.

Watch the orangutan move in the trees and on the ground. They're real swingers in the trees! They're less comfortable walking on the ground.

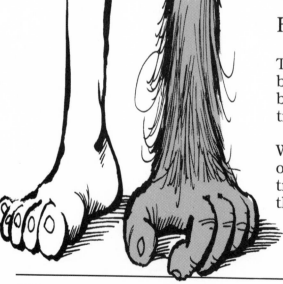

Can You Find an Orangutan's Nest?

Orangutans bend and fold branches to form platforms in the trees. If it rains, they build a roof. Orangutans like things on and over their heads. It makes them feel comfortable. In zoos, some like to carry around a "comfort blanket" made of wool or cotton.

Would an Orangutan Come to Your Party?

No. Orangutans like to be by themselves. Chimps are the real "party animals."

Orangutan Stats

Height: 4 1/2 feet

Weight: 200 lbs.

Arm Span: 8 feet

Tree-Swinging Speed: 3 miles per hour (slow)

Sexually Mature: 6–8 years

Gestation (Pregnancy): 233 days

Life Span: 40–60 years

ZOO CLUES

In the Zoo Shop

• T-shirts and sweat-shirts are the most popular items.
• Lions and tigers are the most popular animals on T-shirts.
• Sea lions, seals, monkeys, giraffes, elephants, and bears are also very popular on T-shirts.
• Children under 10 years old like the zoo's name to be BIG on the shirt.
• Those over 12 years old like the name of the zoo to be small on the shirt.

Zoo Food — For Humans

• 50% of all food sales in the zoo are cold drinks. Every 1 1/2 people buys a soda.
• What is the most popular food item? — ICE CREAM! 20% (1 in 5 visitors) buy ice cream at the zoo.

• Popcorn is almost as popular as ice cream. 18% of the zoo visitors buy it.
• Visitors also gobble up hot dogs (10%), hamburgers (5%), french fries (5%), and cotton candy (3%).

Zoos Do Not Sell

• Objects that the animals may swallow, such as: straws, cones for cotton candy, or balloons.
• Objects that could injure children or the animals, such as: ice cream on sticks, or pennants on pointed sticks.
• Chewing gum — it's too messy.

Zoo Facts

• More than 100 million people visit accredited zoos in North America every year. That is more people than attend all professional football, basketball, and base-ball games combined, each year.
• If all the land of all the zoos in North America was combined, it would fit in an area the size of Brooklyn, New York.
• Almost one-half billion dollars was spent last year on construction of new exhibits and renova-tions of existing facilities.
• It costs about one billion dollars to operate the zoos in North America.
• Almost four million individuals belong to organizations that help support our zoos in North America.

Some Food That the Philadelphia Zoo Buys Every Year

- 8,840 lbs. of bananas
- 1,000,000 crickets
- 2,000,000 mealworms
- 105,000 mice
- 3,000 rats
- 50 snakes (for king cobras and coral snakes that feed on other snakes)
- 312 vials of fruit flies (for the hummingbirds)
- 46,000 lbs. of horsemeat
- 50 gallons of blood (for the vampire bats)
- 15,000 lbs. of dry dog food
- 425,000 lbs. of hay (timothy and alfalfa)

Today's Cooking Lesson:

How to Feed Young Condors
- First, feed a small flock of turkey vultures raw mice, chicken, mackerel, and rats.
- Allow this mixture to "simmer" in the stomach's digestive juices for a few hours.
- Then, show the turkey vultures a net, inspiring them to regurgitate all the excess weight (stomach contents), and flee to the opposite corner of the aviary.
- What they leave behind is scraped up, decorated with a sprig of parsley or orange wheel, and served à la carte to young condors.

Cooking Lesson II:
Bear Soup
- Blend together cod-liver oil, dark Karo syrup, raw eggs, kelp powder, and vitamin powder.
- Make sure that it has the color and consistency of motor oil.
- Pour over a one-half loaf mound of bread. *Yum, yum* — eat 'em up!

Some of the Food Fed to Animals at the San Diego Zoo Every Year.

- 135 rabbits
- 208 pigeons
- 56,000 mice
- 2,500 rats

- 62,240 lbs. of sweet potatoes
- 9,000 lbs. of green beans
- 86 gallons of apricot nectar
- 829 gallons of evaporated milk
- 240 lbs. of yogurt
- 13,500 lbs. of dry dog food
- 2,496 lbs. of applesauce baby food
- 25,575 lbs. of herring
- 464 lbs. of squid

- 410 lbs. of honey
- 715,000 crickets
- 135 tons of alfalfa hay
- 2,825 lbs. of Spanish peanuts

Favorite Snack at the San Diego Zoo (For the Humans)

- The Super Safari Cone!
It is a large, baked, waffle cone filled with ice cream, hot fudge, whipped cream, and topped with candy sprinkles.

"Pigging Out" (Human-Style) at the San Diego Zoo

- 60,000 lbs. of hot dogs sold yearly
- 65,000 lbs. of hamburgers sold yearly
- 280,000 lbs. of french fries sold yearly

Zoo Photo/Video Tips

- Rainy mornings are the best times for pictures. The animals are happy to see you and there are no crowds to get in your way.
- Feeding time is the best opportunity to get pictures of an alert animal.
- After feeding, you can get wonderful "lazy" pictures — of grooming, yawning, stretching, and sleeping animals.
- Study the animals' habits and behavior so that you will discover the best place for your pictures.
- Pick an angle that shows the animals against a natural foreground and background.
- Indoors, to avoid reflections off glass enclosures, place the camera and the flash against the glass.

Zookeeper Quotations

Zookeepers spend more time with the animals than any other people do. They are in some ways members of the animals' extended family. The keepers love and respect their animals and make sure that they are well-fed, clean, and happy. They know their animals so well that they can see signs of illness or unhappiness very early.

More than any other resident in the zoo, the elephants have taught me that all animals have personalities of their own. Elephants act very different at different times. They can be friendly, loyal, curious, upset, frustrated, resourceful, greedy, angry, or frightened. For example, once, a large truck not known to the elephants drove through the zoo in the early morning and scared them. They began to squeal, trumpet, run in circles, and flap their big ears. The elephants ran to us [the keepers] for protection and comfort, just like a young child seeks out his parents when frightened. We did our best to comfort the elephants by petting their trunks and speaking softly to them.

— Dan Maloney, Assistant Curator of Mammals, Philadelphia Zoo

In the wild, animals have two concerns — getting enough to eat and avoiding being eaten by a predator. In the zoo, there are no predators, and a well-balanced diet is provided. So our job is to make the zoo an interesting place to live by providing the animals with family, friends, games, and interesting activities. Gorillas, for example, are kept together in a family group — mother, father, brothers, sisters; have play activities — ropes, balls, boxes to tear up; forage for food treats — popcorn, raisins, and puffed rice.

—Karl Kranz, General Curator of the Philadelphia Zoo

Being with the animals—it's something you never get tired of. It's been all these years, and I still get such a thrill holding a tiger cub, picking up a monkey, petting a giraffe. To be so close to the animals is a real thrill. It hasn't worn off. I don't think it ever will.

—Dr. Carl L. Tinkelman, a dentist for humans who volunteers his time at the Philadelphia Zoo to help keep the animals' teeth and gums healthy. He has done everything from root canals on Siberian tigers to treating pygmy hedgehogs's gum disease.

It is an honor to participate in programs preserving endangered species like the cougar and tiger. We also enjoy talking to and educating the public.

—Al Porta and Steve Cepregi, carnivore keepers at the Philadelphia Zoo

Each one of us carries a share of the responsibilities to keep alive the fascinating and wonderful miracles of life on this planet. We can do this by knowing as much about them as we can.

—Sir Julian Huxley, consulting editor, The Atlas of World Wildlife

111

Index

MICHAEL FOREMAN'S
WORLD OF
FAIRY TALES

ARCADE

FOR THE CHILDREN OF THE WORLD

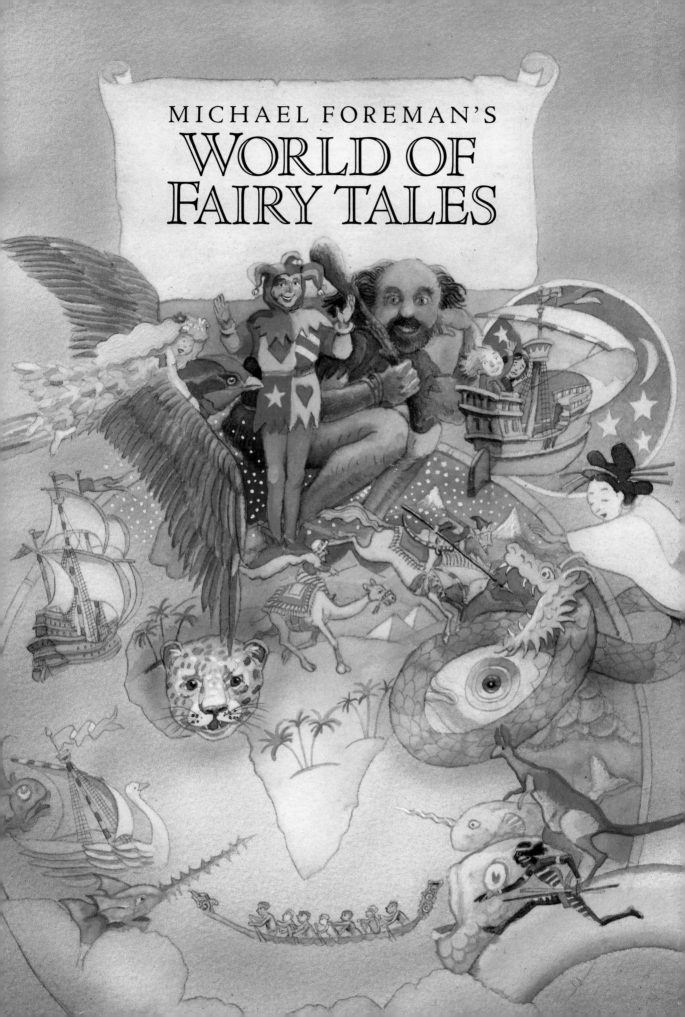

MICHAEL FOREMAN'S
WORLD OF
FAIRY TALES

First U.S. Edition 1991
First published in Great Britain by Pavilion Books Limited

For copyright details of the individual stories see page 144.

ISBN 1-55970-164-1
Library of Congress Catalog Card Number 91-55225
Library of Congress Cataloging-in-Publication information is
available.

Published in the United States by Arcade Publishing, Inc., New York,
a Little, Brown company

10 9 8 7 6 5 4 3 2 1

Designed by Janet James

PRINTED IN ITALY

Contents

AUSTRALIA

Traditional

RETOLD BY DAVID GULPILIL

All the world's peoples have stories of the creation, legends of how the world was formed. The Aboriginals of Australia believe that in the beginning the earth was flat and featureless, without form or colour.

Then came the Dreamtime, a time when giant Beings awoke from their slumbers and travelled the vast grey plains searching for food and burrowing for water. Thus valleys, mountains, ravines and rivers were formed. Many of these features have become sacred sites for the Aboriginals, and one of the most famous is Uluru in the 'red centre' of Australia.

Uluru, or Ayers Rock as it was known for a while, is pitted with shallow caves decorated with secret paintings and the soot of ancient fires. The paintings depict the Dreamtime. A marvellous place to explore alone in the cool dawn. (My tracks from the previous evening had invariably been overlaid by dingo tracks during the night.)

This story tells of the very first sunrise.

Early morning Uluru.

The First Sunrise

Long, long ago in the Dreamtime the earth was dark. There was no light. A huge grey blanket of clouds kept the light and the warmth out. It was very cold and very black. This great grey mass of cloud was very low. So low that the animals had to crawl around. The Emu hobbled, neck bent almost to the ground; the Kangaroo couldn't hop, and none of the birds could fly higher than several feet in the air. Only the Snakes were happy because they, of all the animals, lived close to the ground.

The animals lived by crawling around the damp dark earth, feeling for fruits and berries. Often it was so hard to find food that several days would pass between meals. The Wombat became so tired of people bumping into him that he dug himself a burrow, and learned to sleep for long periods.

Eventually, the birds decided they'd had enough. They called a meeting of all the animals. The Magpies, who were more intelligent than most of the birds, had a plan:

> 'We can't fly because the sky is too low. What we
> need to do, is to raise the sky. If we all gathered
> sticks, then we could use them to push the sky
> up – and then we could fly up with the sky, and
> make lots of room for everyone.'

All the animals agreed it was a good idea, and they set about gathering sticks. The Magpies took a big stick each, and began to push at the sky.

> 'Look, it's going to work!
> The sky! It's moving!'

The Emus and the Kangaroos, the Wombats and the Goannas sat and watched as the Magpies pushed the sky slowly upwards. They used the sticks as levers, first resting the sky on low boulders, then on small hills. As the animals watched, the Magpies, pushing and straining, reached the top of a small mountain.

> 'Munmuck, munmuck, at least we can walk
> about.'

It was still very dark, but at least the Emu could straighten up, and the Kangaroo was able to move in long proud hops.

The Magpies kept pushing the sky higher and higher, until they reached the highest mountain in the whole land. Then with a mighty heave, they gave the sky one last push! The sky shot up into the air, and as it rose it split open and a huge flood of warmth and light poured through on to the land below.

The animals wondered at the light and warmth, but more at the incredible brightly painted beauty of the Sun-Woman. The whole sky was awash with beautiful reds and yellows.

It was the first sunrise.

Overjoyed with the beauty, the light and the warmth, the Magpies burst into song. As their loud warbling carried across the land, the Sun-Woman rose slowly, and began her journey towards the west.

Now, each morning when the Sun-Woman wakes in her camp in the east she lights a fire to prepare the bark torch that she will carry across the sky each day. It is this fire that provides the first light of dawn. As she puts on her paint, the dust from the crushed red ochre colours the early morning clouds a beautiful soft red.

Then she takes up her torch, and begins her daily journey across the sky.

When she reaches the western edge of the world, she extinguishes her flaming bark torch. Then she sits down, and repaints herself in brilliant reds and yellows, ready for her journey through a long underground passage, back to her camp in the east.

So that is why, to this day, every morning when the Sun-Woman wakes and lights her early morning fire, all the magpies greet her with their beautiful, warbling song.

THE ARCTIC

Traditional

RETOLD BY R MALZACK

The Arctic is, I think, the most graphic of regions, white as paper. I remember one particular journey across the North Cape, 38° below, driving by skidoo into a white haze. No horizon, no colour in the sky, no ground. Just blank white, following an old 'winterway' marked by tall twigs stuck in to the snow some distance apart.

Then we saw the reindeer, a vast herd surging like a tide, a brown racing wave breaking over the white hills.

Crossing the North Cape. 1986

How the Raven Brought Light to the World

In the beginning, when the first Eskimos lived in the land of ice and snow, there was light from the sun as we now have it. Then, because the Eskimos were bad, the sun was taken away. People were left on earth for a long time with only the starlight to guide them. The Medicine Men made their strongest charms, but the darkness of night continued.

In one of the Eskimo villages there lived an orphan boy who was allowed to make his home in the community hut. This little boy, like all orphans, had magical powers. He had a special black coat and peaked cap, and when he put them on he changed into a Raven. Then he was able to fly as the Ravens do. When he took off his coat and cap he again turned into a boy.

The village people were good to the little boy, and because he wanted to repay them for their kindness, he went off to search for the sun. He put on his black coat and cap, became a Raven, and flew high up into the air. He flew for many days, and the darkness was always the same. But one day, after he had gone a very long way, he saw a ray of light ahead of him, and he felt encouraged. As he hurried on, the light showed again, plainer than before. At last he came to a large hill. One side of the hill was in bright light while the other side was as black as night. Close to the hill, there was a small house with a man near by.

The boy silently crept closer to the house, until he could look into it. Through the ice window he saw a large ball of fire that glowed with a brilliant light. He had found the sun at last! The boy took off his coat and cap, and began to plan how to get the light away from the man.

After a time, he walked up to the man who was standing outside his house. The man jumped with surprise when he saw the boy, and said, 'Who are you, and where do you come from?'

'It's so dark in our village that I don't like to live there. So I came here to live with you,' said the boy.

'What! All the time?' asked the man.

'Yes,' replied the boy.

'Hmm!' mumbled the man. 'Well, come into the house with me and let's talk it over.' He stooped down, and led the way through the snow tunnel into the house.

The moment the boy was in the house, he snatched up the ball of fire and ran out of the tunnel. He pulled his peaked cap over his face, and turned into a Raven. And he flew as fast as his wings would carry him. When he turned to look behind him, he saw the old man running after him on the ground. The old man cried out, 'Give me my fireball! The Eskimos are bad and they mustn't have it.'

And Raven called back, 'No! Now they're good. They work hard, and need light to hunt and fish.' Then he flew off, holding the sun in his long, clawed feet.

As Raven travelled home, he broke off a piece of the fireball and hurled it through the sky. When it soared over the land of the Eskimos, they rejoiced,

because at last they had daylight again. He went on for a long time in darkness and then sent another piece of the fireball hurtling through the sky, making it day again. This he continued to do at intervals until he reached his village. Once there, he took off his magical coat and cap, and celebrated with the happy villagers.

Nowadays, at Raven's village, day and night follow each other. Sometimes, the nights are very long, because Raven travelled for a long time without throwing a piece of the fireball. And so they have continued. For Raven threw the pieces of fireball with such power that they continue to circle around the land of the Eskimos to this day.

CANADA

Traditional

RETOLD BY CYRIL MACMILLAN

Animals play leading roles in much of the world's treasure of traditional tales. They echo a time when the lives of animal and human were inextricably bound together.

Some North American Indian stories depict an even earlier time, a time when the Americas were inhabited only by the animals. Indeed, the animals were credited with the creation of much that was wonderful, and when the Indians arrived, each group adopted an image of an animal as its totem, a symbol of unity within the group, and with nature.

Caribou and winter sun

Rainbow and the Autumn Leaves

In olden days, long before the Indians came to Canada, all the animals talked and worked like men. Every year after midsummer they held a Great Council at which they were all present. But it happened once in the summer before the council met, that they all wanted to go to the sky to see what the country up there was like. None of them could find a way to go. The oldest and wisest creature on all the earth was Turtle. One day he prayed to the Thunder God to take him to the sky, and his prayer was soon answered. There was a great noise, as if the earth had been split asunder, and when the people next looked for Turtle he was nowhere to be found. They searched everywhere without success. But that evening, when they looked upwards, they saw him in the sky, moving about like a black cloud. Turtle liked the sky so well that he decided to live there always and to send his descendants, later, to the earth. And the sky-people agreed to keep him. They asked him, 'Where do you want to dwell?'

And he answered, 'I should like to dwell in the Black Cloud, in which are the ponds and streams and lakes and springs of water, for I always dwelt near these places when I was young.' So he was allowed to have his wish. But when the Great Council of the animals met on earth in the time of the harvest-moon, he was always present. He came in the Black Cloud, but he always went back to the sky after the Council was ended. And the other animals envied him his good fortune, and they wished that they could go with him.

After a time the animals were greatly distressed and angered by the rumour that a new race of creatures was coming from far over the ocean to inhabit their land. They talked it over very carefully, and they all thought how fortunate it would be if they could all go to the sky with old Turtle, and live like him, free from fear and trouble and care. But they were puzzled to know how to get there, for Turtle had never told any of them the way.

One day Deer, wandering about alone in the forest, as was his custom, came across Rainbow, who often built a path of many colours to the sky. And he said to Rainbow, 'Carry me up to the sky, for I want to see Turtle.'

But Rainbow was afraid to do it, for he wished first to ask the Thunder God for permission, and he put Deer off, and to gain time he said, 'Come to me in winter, when I stay for a time on the mountain near the lake. Then I will gladly carry you to the place where Turtle dwells.'

Throughout the long winter months Deer looked longingly for Rainbow, but Rainbow did not come. Life was growing harder on the earth, and the animals were in terror of the new race that was soon to come to their land, and Deer was very timid and impatient. At last, one day in the early summer, Rainbow came again, and Deer hastened to meet him. 'Why were you false to me?' he asked; 'I waited for you all winter long on the mountain by the lake, but you did not come as you promised. I want to go to the sky now, for I must see Turtle.' Rainbow answered, 'I cannot take you now. But some day, when there is a Fog over the lake, I shall come back to drive it away. Come to me then, and I shall take you to the sky and to the place where Turtle dwells. This time I will not deceive you.'

Rainbow consulted the Thunder God, and received permission to do as Deer wished. Soon afterwards the Fog one day rolled in a thick bank across the lake, and

Deer hurried out to wait for Rainbow. Sure enough, Rainbow came down, as he had promised, to drive the Fog away. He threw his arch of many colours from the lake to the blue hills far away, and the Fog at once disappeared from the place. And he said to Deer, who stood watching him, 'Now I will keep my promise. Follow my many-coloured path over the hills and the forests and the streams, and be not afraid, and you will soon reach Turtle's home in the sky.' Deer did as he was told, and soon he reached the sky. Turtle was glad to see him, and Deer liked the country so well that he decided to stay for ever. And he roamed over the sky everywhere, moving like the wind from place to place.

When midsummer had passed and the harvest-moon had come and the Great Council again met together, Deer was absent for the first time in his life. The animals waited long for him to appear, for they needed his advice, but he did not come. They sent the Birds out to find him. Black Hawk and Woodpecker and Bluejay all sought him in the forest, but they could not find a trace of him. Then Wolf and Fox scoured the woods far and near, but they came back and reported that he could not be found anywhere. At last Turtle arrived at the meeting of the Great Council, as was his custom, coming in his Black Cloud, in which were the ponds and lakes and streams and springs of water. And Bear said, 'Deer is absent from the Council meeting. Where is Deer? We cannot meet without him, for we need his advice.'

And Turtle replied, 'Deer is in the sky. Have you not heard?' Rainbow made a wonderful pathway for him of many varied colours, and by that he came to the sky. There he is now,' and he pointed to a golden cloud scurrying across the sky overhead.

Turtle advised that the animals should all go to the sky to live until they could be sure that the new race of creatures would bring them no harm. And he showed them the pathway that Rainbow had made, stretching from the earth in wonderful colours. The animals all agreed at the Great Council to take Turtle's advice. But they were all very angry at Deer for leaving them without warning, for they thought that all the animals should either stay together faithfully on the earth or go all together to the sky. Bear showed the greatest anger and annoyance. Because of his great strength, he had no fear of the new race that was said soon to be coming, and he had always been inclined to look with scorn on Deer's timid and impatient ways. 'Deer has forsaken us,' he said; 'he deserted us in the hour of our danger, and that is contrary to forest laws and to our code of defence.'

And he thought to himself, 'I shall punish him for this when the time comes.'

In the late autumn, the time agreed upon came for the animals to leave the earth, and Rainbow again made his bright path for them to the sky. Bear was the first to go up because he was the leader, and because with his great weight he wanted to test the strength of the bridge of burning colours over which they had to pass. When he had almost reached the sky, he met Deer on the path waiting to welcome the animals to their new home. And he said to him in anger, 'Why did you leave us behind, without warning, for the land of the Turtle? Why did you desert the Great Council? Why did you not wait until all could come together? You are a traitor to your comrades, and you have been false to our faith.'

And Deer answered, also in anger, 'Who are you to doubt me or my faith? None but the Wolf may ask me why I came or question my fidelity. I will kill you for your insolence.' Deer had grown very proud since he had gone to live in the sky, and he was no longer timid as he had been on earth. His eyes flashed in his fury, and he

18

arched his neck and lowered his antlered head, and rushed madly at Bear to push him from the path.

But Bear was not afraid, for he had often tested his strength with Deer upon the earth. His low, hoarse growls sounded all over the sky, and he prepared to fight. They came together with a shock. For a long time they battled, until the bridge of burning colours trembled and the heavens shook from the force of the conflict. The animals waiting by the lake at the end of the path looked up and saw the battle above them. They feared the results, for they wanted neither Bear nor Deer to die. So they sent Wolf up to the sky to put a stop to the contest. When Wolf reached the combatants, Bear was bleeding freely, for Deer with his antlers had pierced his neck and side. Deer, too, was bleeding where Bear's strong claws had torn a great wound in his head. Wolf soon stopped the battle, and Bear and Deer went away to dress their wounds. Then the other animals went up to the sky over Rainbow's flaming path. And they decided to live in the sky and to send their descendants back to earth when the new race of creatures should come. And they can still sometimes be seen, like clouds hurrying across the sky, in the shape they had on earth.

But the blood of Bear and of Deer dropped from them as they moved to the sky from the scene of their battle along the Rainbow road. It fell freely upon the leaves of the trees beneath them, and changed them into varied colours. And every year when autumn comes in the north country, the leaves take on again the bright and wondrous colours given to them by the blood of Bear and Deer when they fought on the Rainbow path ages and ages ago. And Bear and Deer have never since been friends, and their descendants no longer dwell together in peace, as they did in the olden days.

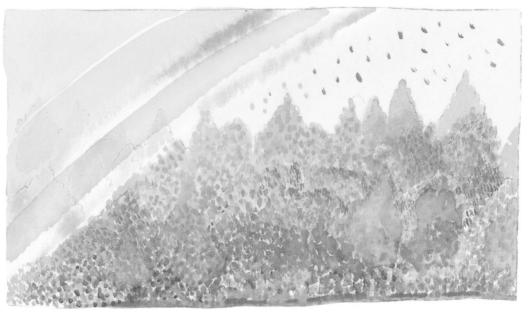

19

CORNWALL

Traditional

RETOLD BY ERIC QUAYLE

Dwarfs, giants, fairies, magicians and witches, monstrous animals and wonders of all sorts are woven together in Celtic legend. For me, as a small child, it was the stories of giants that captured and held my imagination. Perhaps giants have this effect because children are born into a world of giants.

I live much of the time in Cornwall. The huge standing stones dotted about the landscape, and the landscape itself sculpted by tremendous forces, lend weight to the legend: here be Giants.

West Penwith, Cornwall 1986

The Giants of St Michael's Mount

Long, long ago there lived near the village of Marazion a Cornish giant and his wife. His name was Cormoran, and though he was the strongest giant in the land it was his wife Cormelian who was forced to do most of the work. At that time much of the land about was thick forest and Cormoran, despite his great strength, was always fearful that the Cornish peasants whose land and cattle he constantly plundered would one day creep up on him while he was asleep and kill both him and his wife.

He determined to build a hill high enough to see over the forest and beyond, with a castle to top it and windows to see through even when he was lying in his massive oaken bed. And just to make doubly sure he would build his Mount not on land but some way out to sea. No sooner had the idea come to him than he set Cormelian the task of gathering the largest granite boulders she could find, then she was to carry the rocky masses in her apron way out to sea so that first an island and then a mountain would rise up from the seabed. Poor Cormelian worked day after day, lifting the huge granite rocks her husband pointed to with the tree he had shaped into a club, and only occasionally, when the rock he had selected proved too heavy even for the giantess to lift, did he stir himself to give his wife a pull and a heave. Then off she tramped once more, striding with one pace over the wide seashore, then into the sea whatever the state of the tide, deeper and deeper to empty her apron of stones on the ever rising Mount. By late summer the pointed hill of granite could be seen for miles around and Cormoran generously gave his wife a day of rest as he called it, telling her to fetch and carry their furniture and goods and chattels from the deep and gloomy cave they had dwelt in to the summit of the Mount. Then he strode out to sea with his cudgel over his shoulder, sat down on the peak of his island and prepared to conjure his castle from the air. Most giants can perform odd bits and pieces of magic, but for this event Cormoran had saved up his spells for many months, lumping their often tiny scraps of magic into one really big spell and using the entire energy to perform one massive bang. And massive bang it was! From out of a clear blue sky came a clap of thunder which shook houses and cottages from Land's End to the Lizard, and then as frightened villagers streamed out of their homes there it was – on top of the Mount – a castle! A giant's castle,

complete with pinnacles and turrets and narrow slitty windows that Cormoran could peer through and aim his sling-shot at enemies and foes.

'Would the dreaded giant and his wife turn respectable and obey the laws of the land now that they had their own residence?' the villagers asked their elders. But almost before the words were out of their mouths there came a roar from the direction of the Mount and the thud of approaching footsteps that sent them fleeing from their homes. If anything, Cormoran seemed to require even more meat and victuals than ever and he could be seen almost daily wading in two or three steps through the sea to stalk through the meadowland seeking the flocks of sheep and herds of cattle the good folk of Cornwall had reared and cared for. Once found he would pick up as many as three cows at a time, tying their tails together before throwing them over his shoulders while he stuffed sheep by the dozen into the sailcloth bag he carried.

The whole of West Penwith from St Ives to Land's End was in despair, the

villagers knowing they would face a winter of near starvation unless the giant could be killed. Frantically they clubbed together all the gold they had hidden, offering a leather bag heavy with coin to any man brave enough to undertake the task. But out of all the brave men of Cornwall only one young man volunteered. His name was Jack and he lived with his father and mother in a cottage in the village of Ding Dong high up on the moors. His parents begged him not to go, but Jack had made up his mind. Not only that – he had a plan!

That night he went to the seashore opposite the giant's castle and dug in the darkness for many hours until he had made a pit so deep that it was only by the rope ladder whose end he had secured to a rock that he was able to extricate himself. Next he turned to the thin planks of wood he had brought with him, carefully placing them over the pit to form a floor. Finally, he spread sand over the surface so that all looked just as usual. Then he sat himself down to wait.

The sun was high in the sky before Jack saw the massive door of the castle flung

open and Cormoran emerge with his club as big as an oak. He gave his usual roar which could be heard for miles around, but this time to his great surprise there came an answering shout and there was young Jack jumping up and down on the far shore and waving his sword above his head. The giant could hardly believe his eyes, then with a growl of rage he strode savagely across the channel of water raising his massive club as he did so. Instead of running away Jack stood still and even blew a blast on the horn which he carried. This was too much for Cormoran and he took a pace up the beach to squash this puny human with a single blow. As he did so the ground gave way beneath his feet and he was in Jack's pit with only his ugly head sticking out. Quick as a flash Jack ran behind him and with a single blow of his sword lopped off the giant's head.

From the cliffs above him he heard the sound of cheering and looking back he could see the grateful villagers dancing with joy. Suddenly they were silenced as from across the bay came a terrible scream. There was Cormelian, the giant's wife, advancing towards them. As he turned to flee Jack noticed that she seemed smaller than usual and as he gazed she was visibly shrinking. Only magic had kept her and her husband so huge, and with his death the magic was waning and the spell getting weaker and weaker. She was only half way across the water which separated the Mount from the shore and as she shrank the sea came up to her waist, then to her shoulders until, with a final effort she reached shallower waters. But she continued to shrink, smaller than human form now, then the size of a little girl, then as small as a cat, then as a mouse. At that moment a seagull swooped down, picked up the squeaking giantess, and flew off across Mount's Bay. No one ever saw her again.

The villagers once more emerged from behind the rocks where they had watched and waited before, knowing nothing of the hidden pit and thinking that Jack was sure to die. Now, with both giants dead, their joy knew no bounds. The Mayor of Penzance and the Mayor of Marazion, and the Mayor of St Ives, all three came hurrying down the sands with the rest of the grateful Cornishmen to present the hero of the day with his well-earned bag of gold.

That night there were feasts and celebrations throughout all Cornwall and at a special ceremony Jack was given a belt chased with silver on which was written:

> *This is the valiant Cornishman*
> *Who slew the giant Cormoran.*

Jack wore it wherever he went, and that's how he came to be called Jack the Giant-Killer!

Finn's palace was on the top of a hill called Knockmany and it looked out on another mountain called Culamore and there was a deep gorge in between. Finn had settled there so that he could see his enemies a long way off and as well as that he could throw the bodies of his prey into the gorge for the crows to fatten themselves on.

'Oh my bilberry,' said Finn as he saw his wife Oonagh who had plaited her hair and put on a silk dress to please him. At once Finn asked if the reason she had sent for him was true.

''Tis true, Avick,' said Oonagh and went on to tell him how McConigle had pitched tent at the far side of the province and had his famous thunderbolt in the shape of a pancake in his pocket, and called himself The Invincible. Finn put his thumb into his mouth to verify all these things and found that they were true. He could only use his gift of prophecy on very trying and solemn occasions such as this was.

'Finn darling, don't bite your thumb,' said Oonagh very sweetly as she led him into the house where there was a dinner prepared. Finn squatted at one end of the low table, Oonagh at the other and along with maidens to wait on them there were harpists playing in order to soothe Finn. He started by having sixteen duck eggs, eight pig's crubeens and three raw onions for his digestion. The main course was a haunch of roast venison and it was so long that it stretched between them down the length of the table, a sizzling roast dotted with berries and all sorts of herbs. But no matter how much he ate or drank there was a frown on Finn's forehead and a big brown ridge like a furrow on the bridge of his nose because of his thinking.

'Dearest,' said Oonagh as she bobbed along and began to stroke his great naked back. Finn always removed his cloak before he sat down to eat.

'You'll beat him, you always do,' said Oonagh, but Finn shook his head and said it was perilous because according to his thumb he and McConigle had equal strength, ate the same amount of food, weighed the same, and were equally matched in daring, wisdom and cunning.

'What else does it say?' Oonagh asked and Finn put his thumb right inside his mouth and shut his eyes in order to concentrate.

'Take care you don't draw blood,' said Oonagh.

'He's coming,' said Finn, 'he's below in Dungannon,' and at that he jumped up.

'When will he be here?' said Oonagh.

'He'll be here before long,' said Finn and he began to put his vest and his jacket on. He looked at his wife and for the first time she saw fear and apprehension in his eyes. She decided that she would have to help him and make use of her own enchantments. Oonagh was in with the fairies too and with her wand had once turned a hussy into a hound. She told Finn that she would help him to succeed.

'How, how?' said Finn, hitting the table and sending delph in all directions.

Oonagh hurried out of the doorway in order to give a message to her sister who lived on the opposite mountain at Culamore.

'Grania,' said Oonagh, 'are you at home?'

'I'm in the kitchen garden,' said Grania, 'I'm picking berries for a tart.'

'Run up to the top of the hill and look about you and tell us if you see anything untoward,' said Oonagh. They waited for a few minutes with Finn pacing up and down and servants fanning him with great leaves.

'I am there now,' said Grania.

'What do you see?' said Oonagh.

'Oh lawsie me,' exclaimed Grania, 'I see the biggest giant I've ever seen coming out of the town of Dunganoon.'

'What is he like?' said Oonagh.

'He's something terrible to behold,' said Grania and went on to describe a giant of about twelve feet in height, his hair all the way down to his waist, his face ruddy like any giant's except that he had daubed blood over it and, most unnerving of all, his three eyes. He had an eye in the middle of his head that was rolling round like the hands of a clock. Not only was the ground shaking beneath him but the birds in the trees were dying of fright. Along with that he was laughing out loud as if he had just heard the most hilarious joke.

'He's coming up to leather Finn,' said Oonagh to her sister.

'Finn has my sympathy,' said Grania and then she just announced that the giant had picked up a white goat and was wringing its neck and was obviously going to eat it raw.

'I'll tell you what,' said Oonagh, 'call down to him and invite him up to your place for a bite to eat.'

'Why so?' said Finn, unable to follow his wife's drift of thought.

'Strategy,' said Oonagh, 'strategy.'

Grania called across to say she'd be glad to oblige and she'd entertain the monster but she was a bit short of bacon and of butter.

'I'll fling you some across,' said Oonagh and she snapped her fingers for a servant to bring a flitch of bacon and a firkin of butter. However, before throwing them she forgot to say her charms and didn't the butter and the bacon fall into a stream and get carried away.

'Never mind,' said Grania, 'I'll give him heather soup and I'll put shredded bark in it to give him indigestion.'

'Good on you,' said Oonagh and she winked at Finn.

'He'll skewer me,' said Finn.

'Don't be ridiculous,' said Oonagh although to tell you the truth she could see a situation where she herself might be a dainty morsel, a little fritter for the giant's supper.

'My courage is leaving me, I'll be disgraced,' said Finn.

'Two heads are better than one,' said Oonagh as she went towards the place where she kept her magic threads. She drew nine woollen threads of different colours, she plaited them into three plaits, with three colours in each one; she put a plait on her right arm, another round her right ankle, a third round her heart, and in that way Oonagh was protected. Then she got going. She asked the servants to go up in the loft and bring down iron griddles and a child's cradle. She got them to make cakes but she hid the griddles inside the cakes and then baked them in the fire in the usual way. When they were done she dusted them over with flour so as to hide any protuberances and she put them on the window to cool. Then she put down a large pot of milk which she later made into curds and whey and showed Finn how to pick up a curd in his hand and make it smooth as a stone. Then she got a nightgown and a shawl and dressed Finn in it and put a nightcap on his head. She told him that he would have to get into the cradle and completely cover himself with clothes, with only his two eyes peering out.

'I can't fit in a cradle,' said Finn.

'You'll have to double up,' said Oonagh.

'I'll have to triple up,' said Finn as she pushed him towards it.

'You must pass for your own child,' said Oonagh.

'But I'm not a child,' said Finn and he was afraid that he had taken the cowardice too far. Oonagh ignored his mutterings and just put him into the cradle and covered him up with great wool blankets and red deerskins.

'What do I do?' said Finn.

'Whist,' said Oonagh because they could hear the bruiser coming up the hill and giving a skelp of his axe to the dogs to shut them up. He strutted across the courtyard and when he arrived at their door he put a hand around either oak pillar and bellowed 'Anyone home?'

Oonagh came forward all shy and mincing and gave a little gasp to signify to him how formidable he was. He had rat skins and coon skins dangling from his ears and his third eye was rolling about like a spinning top.

'Mr McConigle,' said Oonagh.

'The great McConigle,' said the giant and then asked if he was in the house of Finn.

'Indeed you are,' said Oonagh and gestured towards a chair to make him welcome.

'You're Mrs Finn I suppose,' said the giant.

'I am,' said she, 'and a proud wife at that.'

'Thinks he's the toughest giant in Ireland,' said McConigle.

'It's a proven fact,' said his wife proudly.

'There's a man within three feet of you that's very desirous of having a tussle with him,' said McConigle and he looked around in order to sniff out his rival.

'Is he hiding from me?' he asked.

'Hiding?', said Oonagh. 'He left here frothing, he's gone out to find you and it's lucky for you you didn't meet him, or you'd be a dead man now, your head on his pike as an ornament.'

'You vixen,' said McConigle and he roared with rage but Oonagh was in no way dismayed.

'He's twice your height and much better built,' said she.

'You don't know my strength,' said McConigle.

'In that case would you turn the house,' said Oonagh.

The giant stood up, put his middle finger in his mouth, thought for an instant, then went out, put his arms around the house, picked it up and put it facing a different way. Finn in his cradle was now facing in a different direction and there was sweat pouring out of him with heat and nerves.

'You're a handy giant,' said Oonagh and then told him that she was short of water, but that there was a fine spring under some rocks and that if he could split the rocks she'd be most obliged. He took his axe out from under his leather apron, struck at the rocks and tore a cleft that was hundreds of feet deep. Oonagh began to have doubts.

'Come in and eat,' said she and added that although her husband would make mince of him, the laws of hospitality must be observed.

She placed before him six cakes of the bread and a mound of newly churned butter and she sat down pretending to be polite. He put one of the cakes in his mouth, took a bite and let out the most terrible growl.

'What kind of bread is this,' he said fiercely.

'Fresh bread,' said Oonagh, cool as a breeze.

'And here are two teeth of mine gone,' said he as he hauled out two big molars that were grey in colour and shaped like drinking horns.

'Why,' said Oonagh, 'that's Finn's bread, the only bread that he eats, him and the child there.' At that she offered another cake. As soon as he put it in his mouth another great crack was heard and he let out a yell far fiercer than the first, so that the baby mewled. 'Thunder and giblets,' said he as he pulled out two more teeth with bits of gum on them.

'Well, Mr McConigle,' said Oonagh, 'if you can't manage the bread, don't bother with it but don't be disturbing my child.'

'Mammy, mammy, can I have some bread,' said the baby from the cradle and its voice gave McConigle a start. Oonagh very cleverly handed a cake that had no griddle in and McConigle was flabbergasted as he watched the child gobble it up.

'I'd like to take a glimpse at that lad in the cradle,' said he.

'Certainly,' said Oonagh and she told the little baby to get up and prove himself the worthy child of his father. Now the baby stood up, looked at McConigle and said 'Are you as strong as me?'

'Thundering giblets,' said McConigle, 'how dare you insult me.'

'Can you squeeze water out of a stone?' said the child, and he put a stone into McConigle's hand. McConigle squeezed and squeezed but not a drop of liquid came out.

'Watch me,' said the child and he put his hands under the covers, took out one of the white curds that looked exactly like a stone and squeezed until the liquid came out in a little shower from his hands.

'My daddy is training me,' said he, 'but I have a lot to learn yet.'

McConigle was speechless.

'I'll go back to sleep now,' said the child, 'but I'd hate to waste my time on anyone that hasn't my daddy's strength, that can't eat daddy's bread or squeeze water out of a stone.' Then he slipped down and as Oonagh was pulling the covers up over him he raised his index finger and gave a word of warning to McConigle. 'I'd be off out of here if I were you as it's in flummery my father will have you.'

'What he says is a fact,' said Oonagh as she tucked Finn into the cradle and patted him to let him know how proud she was.

'I'm thinking it is,' said McConigle.

'You're not in his league at all,' said Oonagh and went on to remind McConigle that if the child was that strong he could only guess at the immensity of the father.

'Will you let me feel the teeth of that infant?' said he still in a quandary.

'By all means,' said Oonagh and she took his hand and she stuck it straight into Finn's mouth explaining that the child's best teeth were in the back of his head. McConigle was amazed to find a baby with a full set of grinders and more amazed when he felt something snap and then felt his finger detach itself and when he pulled out his hand there was a big wound where his finger of knowledge had been. Finn had eaten it. So shocked was he and so horror-stricken that he fell down. Finn rose from the cradle and laid roundly on the monster with his bare hands. He could easily have killed him with his sword but that McConigle begged for his life and Finn being a chivalrous hero gave it to him. After that McConigle made his peace, picked up his teeth and his accoutrements and promised to go home to Scotland and never set foot in Ireland again.

RUSSIA

Traditional

RETOLD BY ARTHUR RANSOME

On my first visit to Russia I travelled the length of the Trans-Siberian Railway. I took books to read on the journey but they remained unopened in my bag. I was glued to the train window. The forest went on for days, dotted with wooden villages with small churches and hay ricks.

The track was fringed by an endless ribbon of lupins. On a green hillside girls with flowers in their hair were garlanding cows. Suddenly the forest stopped, and there were days and nights of rolling steppes and lakes like fallen bits of sky.

The Russian tales grow straight out of those dark forests and the open endless steppe. The rivers run with spirits and the deep cold lakes make you shiver with anticipation.

Three days in Moscow. Tree-lined and litter-free, dotted with beautiful churches and quiet back streets and leafy gardens, little traffic, large hotels and grant suits.

Moscow 1970

The Fool of the World and the Flying Ship

There were once upon a time an old peasant and his wife, and they had three sons. Two of them were clever young men who could borrow money without being cheated, but the third was the Fool of the World. He was as simple as a child, simpler than some children, and he never did anyone a harm in his life.

Well, it always happens like that. The father and mother thought a lot of the two smart young men; but the Fool of the World was lucky if he got enough to eat, because they always forgot him unless they happened to be looking at him, and sometimes even then.

But however it was with his father and mother, this is a story that shows that God loves simple folk, and turns things to their advantage in the end.

For it happened that the Tzar of that country sent out messengers along the highroads and the rivers, even to huts in the forest like ours, to say that he would give his daughter, the Princess, in marriage to anyone who could bring him a flying ship – ay, a ship with wings, that should sail this way and that through the blue sky, like a ship sailing on the sea.

'This is a chance for us,' said the two clever brothers; and that same day they set off together, to see if one of them could not build the flying ship and marry the Tzar's daughter, and so be a great man indeed.

And their father blessed them, and gave them finer clothes than ever he wore himself. And their mother made them up hampers of food for the road, soft white rolls, and several kinds of cooked meats, and bottles of vodka. She went with them as far as the highroad, and waved her hand to them till they were out of sight. And so the two clever brothers set merrily off on their adventure, to see what could be done with their cleverness. And what happened to them I do not know, for they were never heard of again.

The Fool of the World saw them set off, with their fine parcels of food, and their fine clothes, and their bottles of vodka.

'I'd like to go too,' says he, 'and eat good meat, with soft white rolls, and drink vodka, and marry the Tzar's daughter.'

'Stupid fellow,' says his mother, 'what's the good of your going? Why, if you were to stir from the house you would walk into the arms of a bear; and if not that, then the wolves would eat you before you had finished staring at them.'

But the Fool of the World would not be held back by words.

'I am going,' says he. 'I am going. I am going. I am going.'

He went on saying this over and over again, till the old woman his mother saw there was nothing to be done, and was glad to get him out of the house so as to be quit of the sound of his voice. So she put some food in a bag for him to eat by the way. She put in the bag some crusts of dry black bread and a flask of water. She did not even bother to go as far as the footpath to see him on his way. She saw the last of him at the door of the hut, and he had not taken two steps before she had gone back into the hut to see to more important business.

No matter. The Fool of the World set off with his bag over his shoulder, singing as he went, for he was off to seek his fortune and marry the Tzar's daughter. He was sorry his mother had not given him any vodka; but he sang merrily for all that. He would have liked white rolls instead of the dry black crusts; but, after all, the main thing on a journey is to have something to eat. So he trudged merrily along the road, and sang because the trees were green and there was a blue sky overhead.

He had not gone very far when he met an ancient old man with a bent back, and a long beard, and eyes hidden under his bushy eyebrows.

'Good day, young fellow,' says the ancient old man.

'Good day, grandfather,' says the Fool of the World.

'And where are you off to?' says the ancient old man.

'What!' says the Fool; 'haven't you heard? The Tzar is going to give his daughter to anyone who can bring him a flying ship.'

'And you can really make a flying ship?' says the ancient old man.

'No, I do not know how.'

'Then what are you going to do?'

'God knows,' says the Fool of the World.

'Well,' says the ancient, 'if things are like that, sit you down here. We will rest together and have a bite of food. Bring out what you have in your bag.'

'I am ashamed to offer you what I have here. It is good enough for me, but it is not the sort of meal to which one can ask guests.'

'Never mind that. Out with it. Let us eat what God has given.'

The Fool of the World opened his bag, and could hardly believe his eyes. Instead of black crusts he saw fresh white rolls and cooked meats. He handed them out to the ancient, who said, 'You see how God loves simple folk. Although your own mother does not love you, you have not been done out of your share of the good things. Let's have a sip at the vodka. . . .'

The Fool of the World opened his flask, and instead of water there came out vodka, and that of the best. So the Fool and the ancient made merry, eating and drinking; and when they had done, and sung a song or two together, the ancient says to the Fool:

'Listen to me. Off with you into the forest. Go up to the first big tree you see. Make the sacred sign of the cross three times before it. Strike it a blow with your little hatchet. Fall backwards on the ground, and lie there, full length on your back, until somebody wakes you up. Then you will find the ship made, all ready to fly. Sit you down in it, and fly off whither you want to go. But be sure on the way to give a lift to everyone you meet.'

The Fool of the World thanked the ancient old man, said good-bye to him, and went off to the forest. He walked up to a tree, the first big tree he saw, made the sign of the cross three times before it, swung his hatchet round his head, struck a mighty blow on the trunk of the tree, instantly fell backwards flat on the ground, closed his eyes, and went to sleep.

A little time went by, and it seemed to the Fool as he slept that somebody was jogging his elbow. He woke up and opened his eyes. His hatchet, worn out, lay beside him. The big tree was gone, and in its place there stood a little ship, ready and finished. The Fool did not stop to think. He jumped into the ship, seized the tiller, and sat down. Instantly the ship leapt up into the air, and sailed away over the tops of the trees.

The little ship answered the tiller as readily as if she were sailing in water, and the Fool steered for the highroad, and sailed along above it, for he was afraid of losing his way if he tried to steer a course across the open country.

He flew on and on, and looked down, and saw a man lying in the road below him with his ear on the damp ground.

'Good day to you, uncle,' cried the Fool.

'Good day to you, Sky-fellow,' cried the man.

'What are you doing down there?' says the Fool.

'I am listening to all that is being done in the world.'

'Take your place in the ship with me.'

The man was willing enough, and sat down in the ship with the Fool, and they flew on together singing songs.

They flew on and on, and looked down, and there was a man on one leg, with the other tied up to his head.

'Good day, uncle,' says the Fool, bringing the ship to the ground. 'Why are you hopping along on one foot?'

'If I were to untie the other I should move too fast. I should be stepping across the world in a single stride.'

'Sit down with us,' says the Fool.

The man sat down with them in the ship, and they flew on together singing songs.

They flew on and on, and looked down, and there was a man with a gun, and he was taking aim, but what he was aiming at they could not see.

'Good health to you, uncle,' says the Fool. 'But what are you shooting at? There isn't a bird to be seen.'

'What!' says the man. 'If there were a bird that you could see, I should not shoot at it. A bird or a beast a thousand versts away, that's the sort of mark for me.'

'Take your seat with us,' says the Fool.

The man sat down with them in the ship, and they flew on together. Louder and louder rose their songs.

They flew on and on, and looked down, and there was a man carrying a sack full of bread on his back.

'Good health to you, uncle,' says the Fool, sailing down. 'And where are you off to?'

'I am going to get bread for my dinner.'

'But you've got a full sack on your back.'

'That – that little scrap! Why, that's not enough for a single mouthful.'

'Take your seat with us,' says the Fool.

The Eater sat down with them in the ship, and they flew on together, singing louder than ever.

They flew on and on, and looked down, and there was a man walking round and round a lake.

'Good health to you, uncle,' says the Fool. 'What are you looking for?'

'I want a drink, and I can't find any water.'

'But there's a whole lake in front of your eyes. Why can't you take a drink from that?'

'That little drop!' says the man. 'Why, there's not enough water there to wet the back of my throat if I were to drink it at one gulp.'

'Take your seat with us,' says the Fool.

The Drinker sat down with them, and again they flew on, singing in chorus.

They flew on and on, and looked down, and there was a man walking towards the forest, with a faggot of wood on his shoulders.

'Good day to you, uncle,' says the Fool. 'Why are you taking wood to the forest?'

'This isn't simple wood,' says the man.

'What is it then?' says the Fool.

'If it is scattered about, a whole army of soldiers leaps up out of the ground.'

'There's a place for you with us,' says the Fool.

The man sat down with them, and the ship rose up into the air, and flew on, carrying its singing crew.

They flew on and on, and looked down, and there was a man carrying a sack of straw.

'Good health to you, uncle,' says the Fool; 'and where are you taking your straw?'

'To the village.'

'Why, are they short of straw in your village?'

'No; but this is such straw that if you scatter it abroad in the very hottest of the summer, instantly the weather turns cold, and there is snow and frost.'

'There's a place here for you too,' says the Fool.

'Very kind of you,' says the man, and steps in and sits down, and away they all sail together, singing like to burst their lungs.

They did not meet anyone else, and presently came flying up to the palace of the Tzar. They flew down and cast anchor in the courtyard.

Just then the Tzar was eating his dinner. He heard their loud singing, and looked out of the window and saw the ship come sailing down into his courtyard. He sent his servant out to ask who was the great prince who had brought him the flying ship, and had come sailing down with such a merry noise of singing.

The servant came up to the ship, and saw the Fool of the World and his companions sitting there cracking jokes. He saw they were all moujiks, simple peasants, sitting in the ship; so he did not stop to ask questions, but came back quietly and told the Tzar that there were no gentlemen in the ship at all, but only a lot of dirty peasants.

Now the Tzar was not at all pleased with the idea of giving his only daughter in

marriage to a simple peasant, and he began to think how he could get out of his bargain. Thinks he to himself, 'I'll set them such tasks that they will not be able to perform, and they'll be glad to get off with their lives, and I shall get the ship for nothing.'

So he told his servant to go to the Fool and tell him that before the Tzar had finished his dinner the Fool was to bring him some of the magical water of life.

Now, while the Tzar was giving this order to his servant, the Listener, the first of the Fool's companions, was listening and heard the words of the Tzar and repeated them to the Fool.

'What am I to do now?' says the Fool, stopping short in his jokes. 'In a year, in a whole century, I never could find that water. And he wants it before he has finished his dinner.'

'Don't you worry about that,' says the Swift-goer, 'I'll deal with that for you.'

The servant came and announced the Tzar's command.

'Tell him he shall have it,' says the Fool.

His companion, the Swift-goer, untied his foot from beside his head, put it to the ground, wriggled it a little to get the stiffness out of it, ran off, and was out of sight almost before he had stepped from the ship. Quicker than I can tell it you in words he had come to the water of life, and put some of it in a bottle.

'I shall have plenty of time to get back,' thinks he, and down he sits under a windmill and goes off to sleep.

The royal dinner was coming to an end, and there wasn't a sign of him. There were no songs and no jokes in the flying ship. Everybody was watching for the Swift-goer, and thinking he would not be in time.

The Listener jumped out and laid his right ear to the damp ground, listened a moment, and said, 'What a fellow! He has gone to sleep under the windmill. I can hear him snoring. And there is a fly buzzing with its wings, perched on the windmill close above his head.'

'This is my affair,' says the Far-shooter, and he picked up his gun from between his knees, aimed at the fly on the windmill, and woke the Swift-goer with the thud of the bullet on the wood of the mill close by his head. The Swift-goer leapt up and ran, and in less than a second had brought the magic water of life and given it to the Fool. The Fool gave it to the servant, who took it to the Tzar. The Tzar had not yet left the table, so that his command had been fulfilled as exactly as ever could be.

'What fellows these peasants are,' thought the Tzar. 'There is nothing for it but to set them another task.' So the Tzar said to his servant, 'Go to the captain of the flying ship and give him this message: "If you are such a cunning fellow, you must have a good appetite. Let you and your companions eat at a single meal twelve oxen roasted whole, and as much bread as can be baked in forty ovens!" '

The Listener heard the message, and told the Fool what was coming. The Fool was terrified, and said, 'I can't get through even a single loaf at a sitting.'

'Don't worry about that,' said the Eater. 'It won't be more than a mouthful for me, and I shall be glad to have a little snack in place of my dinner.'

The servant came, and announced the Tzar's command.

'Good,' says the Fool. 'Send the food along, and we'll know what to do with it.'

So they brought twelve oxen roasted whole, and as much bread as could be baked in forty ovens, and the companions had scarcely sat down to the meal before the Eater had finished the lot.

'Why,' said the Eater, 'what a little! They might have given us a decent meal while they were about it.'

The Tzar told his servant to tell the Fool that he and his companions were to drink forty barrels of wine, with forty bucketfuls in every barrel.

The Listener told the Fool what message was coming.

'Why,' says the Fool, 'I never in my life drank more than one bucket at a time.'

'Don't worry', says the Drinker. 'You forget that I am thirsty. It'll be nothing of a drink for me.'

They brought the forty barrels of wine, and tapped them, and the Drinker tossed them down one after another, one gulp for each barrel. 'Little enough,' says he. 'Why, I am thirsty still.'

'Very good,' says the Tzar to his servant, when he heard that they had eaten all the food and drunk all the wine. 'Tell the fellow to get ready for the wedding, and let him go and bathe himself in the bath-house. But let the bath-house be made so hot that the man will stifle and frizzle as soon as he sets foot inside. It is an iron bath-house. Let it be made red hot.'

The Listener heard all this and told the Fool, who stopped short with his mouth open in the middle of a joke.

'Don't you worry,' says the moujik with the straw.

Well, they made the bath-house red hot, and called the Fool, and the Fool went along to the bath-house to wash himself, and with him went the moujik with the straw.

They shut them both into the bath-house, and thought that that was the end of

them. But the moujik scattered his straw before them as they went in, and it became so cold in there that the Fool of the World had scarcely time to wash himself before the water in the cauldrons froze to solid ice. They lay down on the very stove itself, and spent the night there, shivering.

In the morning the servants opened the bath-house, and there were the Fool of the World and the moujik, alive and well, lying on the stove and singing songs.

They told the Tzar, and the Tzar raged with anger. 'There is no getting rid of this fellow,' says he. 'But go and tell him that I send him this message: "If you are to marry my daughter, you must show that you are able to defend her. Let me see that you have at least a regiment of soldiers." ' Thinks he to himself, 'How can a simple peasant raise a troop? He will find it hard enough to raise a single soldier.'

The Listener told the Fool of the World, and the Fool began to lament, 'This time,' says he, 'I am done indeed. You, my brothers, have saved me from misfortune more than once, but this time, alas, there is nothing to be done.'

'Oh, what a fellow you are!' says the peasant with the faggot of wood. 'I suppose you've forgotten about me. Remember that I am the man for this little affair, and don't you worry about it at all.'

The Tzar's servant came along and gave his message.

'Very good,' says the Fool, 'but tell the Tzar that if after this he puts me off again, I'll make war on his country, and take the Princess by force.'

And then, as the servant went back with the message, the whole crew on the flying ship set to their singing again, and sang and laughed and made jokes as if they had not a care in the world.

During the night, while the others slept, the peasant with the faggot of wood went hither and thither, scattering his sticks. Instantly where they fell there appeared a gigantic army. Nobody could count the number of soldiers in it — cavalry, foot soldiers, yes, and guns, and all the guns new and bright, and the men in the finest uniforms that ever were seen.

In the morning, as the Tzar woke and looked from the windows of the palace, he found himself surrounded by troops upon troops of soldiers, and generals in cocked hats bowing in the courtyard and taking orders from the Fool of the World, who sat there joking with his companions in the flying ship. Now it was the Tzar's turn to be afraid. As quickly as he could he sent his servants to the Fool with presents of rich jewels and fine clothes, invited him to come to the palace, and begged him to marry the Princess.

The Fool of the World put on the fine clothes, and stood there as handsome a young man as a princess could wish for a husband. He presented himself before the Tzar, fell in love with the Princess and she with him, married her the same day, received with her a rich dowry, and became so clever that all the court repeated everything he said. The Tzar and the Tzaritza liked him very much, and as for the Princess, she loved him to distraction.

really was. The brothers, not realizing that it was a trick, reluctantly agreed to take Maui with them.

They paddled on for a while and then stopped. Just as they were about to throw over the anchor and start their fishing, Maui said, 'No. Please don't do that because I know a much better place further out, full of fish – all the fish you could want. Just a little while longer and you'll have all your nets filled in half the time.'

The brothers were tempted by this promise of fish and paddled out a little further when Maui stopped them and told them to start fishing. So they threw over their nets which within a few minutes were overflowing. They couldn't believe their luck.

Their boat was lying low in the water with the weight of their catch so the brothers told Maui that they were going to turn back. But Maui said, 'No, it's my turn. I haven't had a chance to do my fishing.'

'But we have enough!' they replied.

'No! I want to do my fishing,' insisted Maui.

With that, he pulled out his special fishing hook made of bone, and asked for some bait. The brothers refused to give him any so Maui rubbed his nose so hard that it began to bleed. Then he smeared the hook with his own blood and threw it over the side.

Suddenly the boat was tossed about, and Maui was thrilled because he was sure he had caught a very big fish. He pulled and pulled. The sea was in a turmoil and Maui's brothers sat in stunned silence, marvelling at Maui's magic strength.

Maui heaved and tugged for what seemed like an age until at last the fish broke the surface. Then Maui and his brothers could see that what he had caught was not a fish but a piece of land, and that his hook was embedded in the doorway of the house of Tonganui, the son of the Sea God.

Maui's brothers couldn't believe their eyes. This beautiful land pulled up from the sea, was smooth and bright, and there were houses on it and burning fires and birds singing. They had never seen anything so marvellous in their whole lives.

Realizing what he had done Maui said, 'I must go and make peace with the gods because I think they are very angry with me. Stay here quietly and calmly, until I return.'

As soon as Maui had gone the brothers forgot his instructions and began to argue for possession of the land.

'I want this piece,' said one.

'No! I claimed it first. It's mine!' shouted another.

Soon the brothers began to slash at the land with their weapons. This angered the gods even more and its smooth surface was gashed and cut. It could never be smoothed out again.

To this day, those cuts and bruises of long ago can still be seen in the valleys and mountains of New Zealand.

AFRICA

Traditional

RETOLD BY BARBARA WALKER

While researching a book on the Arts of West Africa I visited many towns and villages. Market day was always the most important day of the week, and the market in Kano, a town on the southern fringes of the Sahara, was particularly exciting.

Kano is one of the crossroads of Africa, and in addition to all the local produce and cloth and pottery, there was silver and spices from Arabia, bronzes from Benin, big glass beads and wood carving from Nigeria and the Cameroon, and intricate beadwork from the south. Smoke from the potters' fires mixed with the camp fires of the Blue Men, the Tuareg, who would shortly re-cross the desert with their camel caravans.

The story of 'The Boy and the Leopard' tells of such a market, a market in the far off times when there was a closeness between man and the wild animals. Those days have gone, but the markets continue with all their humour and colour.

Kano, Northern Nigeria. The blue dye pits. 1969

The Boy and the Leopard

Long ago and far away there was a wealthy man who had several wives. Of a sudden, this man learned that his town was to be invaded by men from another tribe. Fearing for his life and the lives of those in his family, the man thought long about what he must do to save them all. Finally he decided that he and his family would leave the town under cover of darkness, and seek safety for themselves in the land at the other side of the forest. Accordingly, that night he gathered together his wives and all their children. Packing up whatever possessions they were able to carry, the party started out through the forest.

Now, the man's favourite wife was soon to bear a child, and she found travelling through the forest very difficult. Despite her husband's urging, she walked more and more slowly, until finally she could go not a single step farther.

Her husband halted in his flight, uncertain of what to do about his wife. If he left her there alone, she would without question be torn apart by wild beasts. On the other hand. if he kept the whole party together, travelling only as fast as his wife could go, they would all be captured and enslaved by the enemy tribe. At last he decided that he must leave his wife to face her own fate, and he went off through the forest with the rest of his family.

The following day, a boy was born to the abandoned wife. Taking her baby, the woman went deeper into the forest and found a place safe from the enemy tribe and from wild animals. There she cared for her child, going out from her shelter only to seek food and clothing for herself and the boy. As the boy grew, he played with the small animals of the forest, each day wandering a little farther away from his mother's protection.

One day while he was playing in the forest he found a leopard cub. They approached each other timidly, but soon, as is the way with young creatures, they were good friends. All day they played in a sunny place in the forest, and when the boy had to leave the cub and go back to his mother, he promised the cub that he would return the following day to play with him. At length the two discovered that they had been born the same year and that each had a mother as his sole protection. When the boy seemed fearful that the cub's mother would kill his own mother, the cub promised to kill meat for the boy and his mother so that the woman need not risk her life by going out to hunt.

One day, however, the young leopard came home to find his mother standing over the body of the woman, who had gone out to seek water and had been brought down by the mother leopard. Grief-stricken, the cub went in search of the boy and, telling him what had happened, he promised to take care of the boy so that he would suffer neither hunger nor harm.

After that, he took the boy to live with him in his own cave. Day after day, the two became closer friends, until they almost forgot that one was a leopard and the other a boy.

The cub noticed one day that his friend was very sad. After much coaxing, the boy told the cub what was troubling him. 'Long ago my mother told me that when I was old enough I should offer a sacrifice to the gods so that I might have a life filled with joy and contentment. I am now old enough, but I am unable to get the proper things to offer in sacrifice.'

'What do you need?' asked the young leopard.

'My mother said I must offer snails, kola nuts, and palm nuts. But such things are beyond my means. They are sold in the marketplace. How am I to get the money for such a purpose?' the boy asked sadly.

'Do not worry,' said the leopard. 'I shall go to the market myself and get them for you.' Despite the boy's urging, the cub would not reveal the plan he had for getting the goods from the marketplace.

On the following market day, the leopard arose very early and quietly left the cave. Going to the marketplace, he climbed a tree overlooking the market and hid himself there. By midday, the marketplace was thronged with people. Suddenly the lepoard leaped down into the midst of the crowd. The people fled far and wide in their panic. Calmly the leopard chose those things which the boy needed for his sacrifice and he returned with them to the cave. The next day, the boy offered a sacrifice to appease his gods.

Not long after that, the boy again looked sad. 'What is the matter now, my friend?' the leopard inquired.

The boy sighed. 'I need clothes. But how am I to find something suitable to wear?'

'Clothes?' puzzled the leopard. 'I do not see why you need clothes, my friend, but if you need them, I shall get them for you.' Going to the market on the following market day, the leopard again frightened the crowds away from the stalls and brought back some fine clothes for the boy.

Some time later, the leopard, noting that the boy looked sad and woebegone, asked what was troubling him. The boy sighed deeply. 'My friend,' said he, 'it is the custom among men to marry. But how am I to find a bride?'

But fear is not easily dismissed. Although the girl wished to please her husband, she became steadily more uneasy about the leopard's visits. Finally she slipped away one day to visit her parents, and when they detected that something was troubling her, she wept and told them of her husband's strange friend. Her father at once suspected that this was the animal which had killed his daughter in the marketplace. 'He may be a friend of your husband's, but he is no friend of yours,' her father said. 'The leopard must be destroyed.'

At once the King summoned a dozen of his most trusted palace guards. 'Go this evening at sunset,' he instructed them, 'and lie in wait at the lower end of my daughter's garden until you see a leopard enter. Kill him and return to me.' As for his daughter, he kept her at the palace, where she would be safe until the leopard had been disposed of.

That evening the leopard came a little earler than the usual time. To his surprise, he was met by a shower of poisoned arrows. He ran back toward the forest, but he had been fatally wounded, and shortly afterwards he died. The guards were satisfied that he had been destroyed, and they returned to the palace to carry their report to the king.

When the boy arrived at the appointed place, he was surprised not to see the leopard. A trail of blood led him to the edge of the forest, where his friend lay dead. As the boy knelt to examine the leopard for any faint signs of life, he became aware that some creature was watching him. It was the tortoise, who had chanced to see the close of the leopard's life. Weeping, the boy begged the tortoise to find him one of the magic leaves, that he might restore life to his friend. After much persuasion, the tortoise led him to a plant bearing the magic leaves. Quickly breaking off a leaf, the boy went to the leopard and squeezed a few drops of the juice into his eyes.

As soon as he had opened his eyes, the leopard reproached the boy for his unkind treatment.

'Ah, but I was not the one who shot you,' the boy assured him, 'nor do I know why you were shot.'

'My friends,' the tortoise said, 'do not blame men for this action. Your fellowship does not fit the world of men. And even in the world of animals it is unusual enough so that many will strive to destroy it. The time is past for your friendship. Return each to your own world and be content.'

Cutting a palm branch, the tortoise tore it apart before them in the age-old symbol of separation. Heavy with grief, the leopard turned and went off into the forest. The boy watched sadly until he could no longer see the leopard among the trees. Then he turned and walked through his garden and into the world of men. From that day, men and wild animals ceased to be friends.

TINY TALES

There are very few wasted words in the classic tales. Of course the story-tellers would embellish the bare bones and add local details to suit the listeners, but the inherent sweep and richness is remarkable for such short stories. Great adventures and a lot of good sense are presented in precious few words.

Here is a short story from Tartary followed by two little stories from the Grimm brothers and two by Terry Jones, a modern master of the short epic.

The Leaning Silver Birch

There once lived a man who was poor but as sharp as a bone needle. And in the same aul lived a rich man who thought himself smarter than the night is black.

The rich man was walking along one time when he spotted his neighbour in the distance leaning against a tree.

Coming up to him, he said:

'I have heard you possess the tongue of a magpie and the brain of a fox. But you cannot outwit me!'

'I could do so for sure,' replied the other. 'But not right now: I've left my box of tricks at home.'

The rich man gave a mocking laugh.

'Then run home and fetch it. I'll wait for you . . .'

'I would gladly do so,' replied the other. 'But you see, if I move away from this leaning silver birch, it will fall over.'

The rich man grinned.

'Enough of your excuses! Just go and get your box of tricks. I'll hold up the tree till you get back.'

And off went the quick-witted one, smiling to himself.

In the meantime the boaster waited and waited, holding up the tree. It was only when the villagers gathered to laugh at him that he realized he had been tricked. And never again did he boast about his quick wit.

Whisp of Straw, Lump of Coal, and Little Broad Bean

In a village not far from here there lived a poor old woman who'd got herself a dish of beans and was going to boil them up for her supper. So she made up a fire in the hearth and to hasten it along she used a handful of straw to light it. But when she tipped the beans into the pot one of them fell on the floor without her noticing and came to rest by a bit of the straw. Soon afterwards a glowing lump of coal jumped from the fire down beside the other two.

The whisp of straw opened up a conversation. 'Well now, friends,' he said, 'where have you come from?'

And the lump of coal answered, 'With the greatest of good fortune I've jumped out of that fire. If I hadn't managed to do it I was bound for certain death – I'd have been burnt to ashes.'

And the bean said, 'Yes, me too. I've only just been able to save my skin. If the old woman had tipped me into that pot I'd have been boiled up into mash like all my friends.'

'And would I have had any better fate?' asked the straw. 'That old woman has sent my brothers up in smoke and flames. Sixty of 'em jam-packed to the slaughter, but luckily for me I slipped through her fingers.'

'Well what are we going to do with ourselves?' asked the lump of coal.

'I think,' said the bean, 'that since we've all been lucky enough to escape a nasty death we should become good companions; and for fear of any more disasters overtaking us here we should go on the road together and leave straightaway for another country.'

The other two were pleased with this suggestion and so they all set out. It wasn't long, though, before they came to a little stream, and since there was no bridge or plank across it they had no idea how they were to get to the other side. But the straw was struck with a good idea and said, 'Look here; I'll lie down across the stream and you two can use me as a bridge.' And the straw lay down, stretching himself from one bank to the other, and the lump of coal (who had an impulsive nature) immediately began to scamper over this newly opened bridge. But when he got to the middle and heard the water rushing below him he took fright, stood stock-still and wouldn't trust himself to move an inch further. This caused the straw to catch alight and it broke into two pieces and fell into the stream. The lump of coal tumbled in after, sizzled as it hit the water and then gave up the ghost.

The bean, who had prudently stayed on the bank all this time, couldn't help laughing when he saw what happened. In fact he just couldn't stop, and he laughed so hard that he burst. And that, I'm afraid would have been the end of him except that, to his great good fortune, a travelling tailor was having a rest down there beside the stream. And since this tailor was a kind-hearted fellow he fetched out his needle and thread and sewed the bean together again. The bean thanked him with a great show of gratitude, but because the tailor had sewn him up with black thread, beans from his family have always had a black seam down the middle from that day to this.

Three Raindrops

A raindrop was falling out of a cloud, and it said to the raindrop next to it: 'I'm the biggest and best raindrop in the whole sky!'

'You are indeed a fine raindrop,' said the second, 'but you are not nearly so beautifully shaped as I am. And in my opinion it's shape that counts, and *I* am therefore the best raindrop in the whole sky.'

The first raindrop replied: 'Let us settle this matter once and for all.' So they asked a third raindrop to decide between them.

But the third raindrop said: 'What nonsense you're both talking! *You* may be a big raindrop, and *you* are certainly well-shaped, but, as everybody knows, it's purity that really counts, and I am purer than either of you. *I* am therefore the best raindrop in the whole sky!'

Well, before either of the other raindrops could reply, they all three hit the ground and became part of a very muddy puddle.

The Old Man and his Grandson

There was once a very old man, almost blind and deaf, whose knees and hands trembled. At meal times he could hardly hold his spoon, and often dropped soup on the tablecloth and when he'd taken a spoonful some of it spilled out of his mouth.

His son and his son's wife thought it was disgusting and eventually told him to sit in the corner behind the stove. They gave him his food in an earthenware bowl and never gave him enough. He sat and looked sadly at the table, and he spilled tears into his soup.

One day his old hands trembled so much he dropped his bowl and it smashed to the floor. His son's wife shouted at him and he turned to the corner and sighed.

She bought him a crude wooden bowl for a few copper coins and he had to eat all his meals from it. As they were sitting there one day, the little four-year-old grandson was playing on the floor with some bits of wood.

'What are you doing?' his father asked.

'I'm making a trough,' the child replied, 'for father and mother to drink out of when I'm big.'

Husband and wife stared at each other for a while and then burst into tears. Then they asked the old grandfather back to the table and he ate with them from then on, and even when he spilled a few drops, nobody said anything.

A Fish of the World

A herring once decided to swim right round the world. 'I'm tired of the North Sea,' he said. 'I want to find out what else there is in the world.'

So he swam off south into the deep Atlantic. He swam and he swam far far away from the seas he knew, through the warm waters of the equator and on down into the South Atlantic. And all the time he saw many strange and wonderful fish that he had never seen before. Once he was nearly eaten by a shark, and once he was nearly electrocuted by an electric eel, and once he was nearly stung by a sting-ray. But he swam on and on, round the tip of Africa and into the Indian Ocean. And he passed by devilfish and sailfish and sawfish and swordfish and bluefish and blackfish and mudfish and sunfish, and he was amazed by the different shapes and sizes and colours.

On he swam, into the Java Sea, and he saw fish that leapt out of the water and fish that lived on the bottom of the sea and fish that could walk on their fins. And on he swam, through the Coral Sea, where the shells of millions and millions of tiny creatures had turned to rock and stood as big as mountains. But still he swam on, into the wide Pacific. He swam over the deepest parts of the ocean, where the water is so deep that it is inky black at the bottom, and the fish carry lanterns over their heads, and some have lights on their tails. And through the Pacific he swam, and then he turned north and headed up to the cold Siberian Sea, where huge white icebergs sailed past him like mighty ships. And still he swam on and on and into the frozen Arctic Ocean, where the sea is forever covered in ice. And on he went, past Greenland and Iceland, and finally he swam home into his own North Sea.

All his friends and relations gathered round and made a great fuss of him. They had a big feast and offered him the very best food they could find. But the herring just yawned and said: 'I've swum round the entire world. I have seen everything there is to see, and I have eaten more exotic and wonderful dishes than you could possibly imagine.' And he refused to eat anything.

Then his friends and relations begged him to come home and live with them, but he refused. 'I've been everywhere there is, and that old rock is too dull and small for me.' And he went off and lived on his own.

And when the breeding season came, he refused to join in the spawning, saying: 'I've swum around the entire world, and now I know how many fish there are in the world, I can't be interested in herrings anymore.'

Eventually, one of the oldest of the herrings swam up to him, and said: 'Listen. If you don't spawn with us, some herrings' eggs will go unfertilized and will not turn into healthy young herrings. If you don't live with your family, you'll make them sad. And if you don't eat, you'll die.'

But the herring said: 'I don't mind. I've been everywhere there is to go, I've seen everything there is to see, and now I know everything there is to know.'

The old fish shook his head. 'No-one has ever seen everything there is to see,' he said, 'nor known everything there is to know.'

'Look,' said the herring, 'I've swum through the North Sea, the Atlantic Ocean, the Indian Ocean, the Java Sea, the Coral Sea, the great Pacific Ocean, the Siberian Sea and the frozen Arctic. Tell me, what else is there for me to see or know?'

'I don't know,' said the old herring, 'but there may be something.'

Well, just then, a fishing-boat came by, and all the herrings were caught in a net and taken to market that very day. And a man bought the herring, and ate it for his supper.

And he never knew that it had swum right round the world, and had seen everything there was to see, and knew everything there was to know.

FRANCE

Madame Leprince de Beaumont

RETOLD BY MICHAEL FOSS

Madame Leprince de Beaumont is usually credited as the creator of Beauty and the Beast although she derived the structure from a Madame Gabrielle Susanne Barbot de Gallon de Villeneuve who published a much longer version (well she would, wouldn't she) some twenty years earlier in 1740.

There was, however, an Italian version even earlier than this, and it is likely that this most famous love story had its beginnings much further back and in much humbler circumstances.

The Beast has been depicted in many ways, sometimes hoofed and horned, sometimes as a man with goats' legs or a lion's head or as a serpent. The greatness of the story, however, is that no matter how grotesquely the Beast is portrayed he gains the affection of Beauty and the reader, and there is even a sense of loss at the end when he transforms into just another Prince.

Beauty and the Beast

In a far country, there was a merchant who had once been rich, but fell on hard times. His children, used to the best things, did not like their new life in a poor cottage. They had grown selfish and spoilt, and they complained bitterly. All except one.

She was the youngest, and she was neither selfish nor spoilt. In their little cottage she did the housework while the others complained. And because she was so willing and kind and pretty her father called her Beauty.

Then the merchant heard that a ship which he had thought was lost had now returned. Thinking that his fortune was saved, he prepared to go to the city and asked the children, just as he used to do, what presents he could bring them. The brothers and sisters wanted many expensive and foolish things, but Beauty asked for no present, except to see her father safe home.

'O, do accept something,' her father said. And at last she asked for just one rose.

In the city, the arrival of the lost ship led to bitter arguments. The quarrel was taken to court, but after six months, while the lawyers grew rich, nothing was settled. In mid-winter, the merchant sadly set out for home, as poor as he had ever been. As he went, the snow was falling. In the gloom of the forest he could not find the path and the wolves howled. His horse stumbled, blinded by the weather.

In the night, the merchant almost gave up hope, for it seemed that death was coming to gather him. But next morning, suddenly he found himself in a strange land of sunlight. Instead of snow-covered forest paths he saw an avenue of orange-trees leading through gardens to a castle with towers that reached into the sky. He rode to the door and called but there was no answer. He stabled his horse and entered the castle, going through rooms full of light and treasures and silence. In a far room he found food ready. Then, tired out by his journey, he slept.

When he awoke he was still alone. In the great, silent rooms he could find no one. He walked through the castle and through the gardens, seeing wonderful things on every side, and soon he began to think of his lost wealth and of his family. How happy they would be in this place! And since there seemed to be no one here, why should he not fetch them? Yes, he would do it. So he hurried to the stables, but as he passed through a pathway of roses he remembered his promise to his youngest, dearest child. He stopped and picked a single red rose.

At once, there was a terrible noise and a monstrous Beast stood in the path.

'Did I not,' the frightful thing roared, 'give you the freedom of my castle? How dare you steal my rose. I have a mind to kill you right now.'

The merchant fell on his knees, begging for mercy. He explained his sad story, telling the Beast that the rose was for his daughter Beauty who was so good and kind. The Beast listened, grinding his ugly teeth. But when he spoke again he was not quite so fierce.

'Your life will be saved,' said the Beast, 'if one of your daughters will offer to live with me here. Go now, and let them choose. Return at the end of the month. And do not think you can escape my power.'

The horse seemed to know the way without any guide, but the merchant rode with a heavy heart. At the cottage, his children, who had feared that their father was dead, kissed him and laughed with joy. But when they heard what the Beast had said they were angry and blamed Beauty for wanting the rose. Now they would have to fly to a far land, beyond the reach of the Beast.

But Beauty said: 'Dear father, it is my fault. Come, let us go to the castle. I will stay with the Beast.'

Sadly the merchant agreed, and sadly they returned to the strange castle, standing above the forest so shining and mysterious. They went through the rich, empty rooms and again found a meal made ready. When they were eating they heard

a roaring of wind. The door burst open and the Beast came in like thunder.

'Well, Beauty,' he bellowed, 'have you chosen to stay?'

His looks were terrible to her eyes, but she answered quietly that she would stay.

'Very well, but your father must leave. He may take two trunks of jewels for his family but he must never return. Choose what you like, then wave your father goodbye.'

With many tears she kissed her father goodbye. Then, worn out by sorrow, and by fear for the future, she fell on her bed and slept. She dreamed. She found herself in a golden country of meadows and woods. As she wandered there a handsome Prince appeared and spoke to her in a tender and loving way, begging her to be kind to him.

'Dear Prince,' she sighed, 'what can I do to help you?'

'Be grateful for what you are given,' he replied, 'but do not believe all you see. Above all, do not leave me. Rescue me from my cruel suffering.'

Then the Prince faded away and his place in the dream was taken by a tall, lovely lady, who commanded Beauty: 'Do not sigh for the past. Have faith and do not believe in appearances only. Great things await you in the future.'

Thus began her life in the castle. Each day, she wandered through the rooms and the gardens. She met no one. Hidden hands prepared everything she might need. The days sped by with music and magical entertainments. And every evening, at supper, the Beast came, snorting and twisting his ugly great head.

'Well, Beauty,' he roared, 'are you going to marry me?'

But Beauty shook with fright and tried to creep away. And when the Beast had gone she went quickly to bed and entered the land of dreams where her Prince was waiting.

'Do not be so cruel,' the Prince would beg, 'I love you but you are so stubborn. Help me out of my misery.' He had a crown in his hands, which he offered her, kneeling and weeping at her feet.

But what did this dreaming mean? Beauty did not know. Her days were full of wonders. The sun shone always, and the birds sang. Bands of pretty apes were her servants. But each evening came the Beast, with his grim looks and his terrible question. And each night, in sleep, her Prince sighed for his freedom.

As the days passed, slowly she began to feel sorry for the Beast. He was kind, in his rough way, and gave her everything. Surely his ugliness was not his fault. But she was lonely, too. She saw no one but the Beast. She missed her family. She began to sleep badly. Her dreams were full of worry. Her Prince seemed close to despair.

Then, one night, she dreamed that the Prince ran at the Beast with a dagger, meaning to kill him. Beauty stepped between them, pleading for the Beast, saying that the terrible monster was her friend and protector. The Prince disappeared and at once the tall lady was standing in his place.

'You will soon be happy,' she told Beauty, 'but only if you do not believe in appearances.'

Next morning, waking tired and sad and lonely, she decided to ask the Beast for permission to see her family just once more.

When the Beast heard this he fell to the ground and groaned. But he said he could not deny anything to his Beauty. She could go, and take four chests of treasure with her. But if she did not return after two months, her Beast would die.

Her family were amazed to see her. Her father laughed and cried to have his favourite daughter back. And the four chests of treasure made even her brothers and sisters forget their troubles. They all begged her not to go back to the castle, and for a while she was so happy with her family that she never thought of the Beast.

Two months went by without her notice. Then, one night, she had another dream. She dreamed that she saw the Beast at the point of death. At once, she awoke. She remembered a ring that the Beast had given her, and turning it on her finger she was carried in a flash to the castle. She ran through the great, silent rooms but there was no sign of the monster. She dashed into the gardens and the park, calling his name, running here and there. At last, when night had fallen, she stumbled on his still body in the moonlight.

'Dear Beast,' she cried, 'are you dead? O, please forgive me. I never realized before that I love you. Now I fear I have killed you.'

But his heart was still beating and her presence began to revive him. In a while he was able to stagger to the castle. As he lay on a sofa, she heard him whisper in his sad, growling voice.

'Beauty, have you come back to me? Will you marry me now?'

And she answered at once: 'Yes, dear Beast.'

Then there was a blaze of lights, and loud music, and the Beast vanished. Instead, before her stood the Prince of her dreams, with the tall lady beside him. Beauty and the Prince took hands, and the lady smiled and blessed them.

'You have rescued my son,' she told Beauty, 'from the evil magic that has imprisoned him for so long in the hideous body of the Beast. When you chose him freely, you released the Prince from the spell. Now you will marry him. No longer will you be Beauty and the Beast, but the Prince and Princess of all this great and lovely land.'

ARABIA

Traditional

RETOLD BY AMINA SHAH

The storyteller is still found today in many Arab speaking countries. In the market place in Marrakesh, for instance, where there are acrobats and snake charmers, the largest and most attentive crowd surrounds the storyteller. The nearby queue for the open air dentist hangs on every word.

The listeners range from the oldest hearing the stories for the umteenth time to the youngest child possibly hearing them for the first. Here there are no children's stories and adult stories, only good stories. The weak stories were forgotten long ago.

Near the Valley of the Kings 1976

The Princess and the Mouse

Once upon a time there lived the daughter of a king. Her name was Safia. Her father and mother loved her very much, and would deny her nothing in the world.

One day, a magician came to the palace and asked for sanctuary, saying that he was a professor who was being persecuted by his enemies and had nowhere to write an important book.

'Good professor,' said the King, 'you shall have a room placed at your disposal and everything that you desire, in order that you may finish your great work.'

So the magician went on with his spells and magic formulas, pretending to be engrossed in scholarly matters. Every Friday, which was the day of rest in that far land, the magician paid his respects to the King and his court, but secretly he desired to take away the King's throne.

One day he disguised himself as an old woman and walked under the trees in the palace gardens till he met Safia.

'Princess,' he said, 'let me be your laundress, for I can wash linens and silks as finely as anyone in the world, and I would do it for almost nothing if I could serve Your Highness.'

'Good woman,' said the Princess Safia, 'I can see that you are a poor creature and grieve for your condition. Come to my private quarters and I shall give you some of my linen to wash.'

So the disguised magician followed the princess into the palace, and before the girl could see what was happening he bundled her into a laundry bag and ran away as fast as his legs would carry him. He took the Princess into his private room. Muttering a magic spell, he made her as small as a doll, and put her in a cupboard.

The next Friday he went to the court as usual, and found the whole palace in uproar. 'The Princess Safia has vanished, and His Majesty is nearly out of his mind. All the soothsayers have tried to find out through their magical powers where she can be, but none of them have managed it,' said the Grand Vizier.

The wicked magician smiled, for he knew that his spell was so strong it would defy all the soothsayers in the land until the day of his death.

The next day passed, and the Queen was weeping in her bower when the magician entered, disguised as a washer-woman. He put her into a laundry bag and took her into his private room. She was turned into a doll no bigger than his thumb.

'Ha-hah!' laughed the magician, 'I will now go and capture the King, and will rule the country myself.'

So, next day, he waited until the King had gone to rest, tired out with worrying about the Queen's disappearance, and disguised in his usual way, he captured the King also. He turned the King into a doll no bigger than the Queen, and shut him up in the cupboard too.

Now, with their royal family gone, all the courtiers began to weep and wail, and came to the magician's study in a large party to beg for his advice.

'You are a learned man,' said the Grand Vizier, 'you must know a lot of things. Will you please tell us what to do?'

'Until your King and Queen and Princess come again, let me be your ruler,' said the magician, and the people agreed. So for a long time the wicked magician ruled over the people and gathered much wealth, for they brought him all the gold in the country. Every now and again he would send out troops to search the length and breadth of the land for news of the missing King and his wife and daughter. But, of course, there was no sign of them.

Now, one day a mouse found its way into the cupboard where the Princess Safia was hidden, and got the surprise of its life when she said, 'Mouse, mouse, eat a hole in this cupboard so that I can escape, for the wicked magician who turned me into this shape will never let me out, and I shall die.'

'Who are you?' asked the mouse.

'My father is the King, and will reward you handsomely. You shall have free cheese for the rest of your life,' said the Princess.

'Allah have mercy!' said the mouse. 'His Majesty the King has disappeared, and so has the Queen, and the magician is on the throne.'

'Oh no,' wept the Princess, 'what has happened to them? Can the wicked magician have captured them too?'

'Wait here,' said the mouse, 'and I will have a look in the rest of the cupboard.' And sure enough, he found the King and Queen, turned into tiny dolls, on the top shelf. But in their case they were stiff as if they had been carved out of wood, because the magician had cast a different spell upon them.

The mouse went back and told the Princess the sad news.

'Alas, alas,' the Princess cried, 'what am I to do then, for even if I do escape what will happen to me?'

'Princess,' said the mouse, 'I will help you. I will go and see a Wise Woman who lives in a hollow tree, and tonight I shall come back and tell you what she says.'

So the Princess hid once more in the cupboard, and the mouse scuttled off.

Inside a large tree which had seen many winters there lived an old Wise Woman, and the mouse went to her, saying 'Mother, tell me what I should do to help the King's daughter who has been turned into a doll by the magician. She hopes to

escape through a hole I shall nibble in a cupboard door. I have discovered that our missing King and Queen are also in the same cupboard, turned into wooden dolls no bigger than your thumb.'

'Tell the King's daughter that she must come here when the moon is up and I will help her,' said the Wise Woman.

The mouse went back when it was night and nibbled the wood away until it was possible for Safia to get through the hole. As she was so small, it was easy for the Princess to run with the mouse out of the palace without being seen by the guards. When the moon rose and the garden was flooded with light, the tiny Princess went to a cavity in the tree which the mouse had showed her, and peeped in.

'Enter, King's daughter,' said the Wise Woman. 'I have found out by looking in my magic books the answer to your problem.' The mouse waited nearby to see that no one was coming, and Safia sat on a footstool as the old woman read from a large volume of magic.

'You must go on until you reach the crossroads, and in a field near by you will see an orange-coloured horse, already saddled and bridled for a journey. Jump on his back, after giving him a magic grass-seed to eat.'

'Where shall I get the magic grass-seed?' asked the Princess.

'I will give it to you,' said the Wise Woman, looking into a drawer.

'What am I to do after I have caught the horse?' asked Safia.

'King's daughter, you must whisper into his ear, "Take me, Orange Horse, to where the sacred pear tree grows, so that I may bring away a pear from its topmost branch," ' said the old woman, putting her book back on the shelf.

'And then shall I regain my proper size?' asked the Princess.

'When the wicked magician is dead and not before shall you turn back into your normal size,' said the Wise Woman. 'You must mount the orange horse's back once more and ride until you reach the Well of the Green Ogre. Whisper into the horse's right ear and you will arrive there before you know it. Drop the pear right into the depths of the well, for the wicked magician's soul is hidden in that pear, and if it falls into the ogre's den it will be devoured by the ogre, and the magician will die.'

'What will happen then?' the Princess wanted to know.

'After that, all the creatures turned into other shapes by the magician will return to their own forms, and all will be as it was before.' And the Wise Woman put a grass-seed into her hand.

So the tiny Princess thanked the Wise Woman, said good-bye to the mouse, and ran on in the moonlight until she reached the crossroads.

She saw, just as the old woman had said, a horse which was the colour of an orange, with a beautiful golden mane and tail, standing in the field, ready saddled and bridled.

'Orange Horse! Orange Horse!' called Safia in a low voice. 'Here is a magic grass-seed. Take me to the tree where the sacred pears grow, so that I may pick the topmost pear from its branches.'

So the orange-coloured horse put its head down close to Safia, and she held out the seed, which he swallowed. Then he put his head down again so that she could climb on to his neck, clinging to the golden mane. Soon she was hanging on to the saddle for all she was worth. The horse neighed twice, then, tossing his head, galloped away like the wind.

In less time than it takes to tell, Safia found herself in a beautiful orchard where there were cherry trees, plum trees, and trees with mulberries upon them, but only one pear tree.

'Here it is,' said the horse; and standing on the saddle Safia stretched up into the branches. She picked a pear from the topmost branch and put it carefully into the saddlebag.

'Take me to the Well of the Green Ogre,' she whispered in the horse's right ear. The orange-coloured horse nodded and was off like the wind, his hooves moving so

fast they seemed never to touch the ground. There, beside three palm trees, was a well. In the moonlight Safia saw that just inside the well there was an ogre's head as big as a pumpkin, with huge round eyes and a large mouth. She hurriedly took the pear containing the soul of the magician out of the saddlebag and dropped it right into the Green Ogre's mouth. Instantly he chewed the pear up into tiny pieces, and Safia suddenly found herself growing. She was her own size again – the wicked magician was dead.

The horse took her back to the crossroads, and just as she was about to thank him, there was a clap of thunder and he disappeared before her eyes.

She hurried to the palace, and then to the room where she knew her mother and father were imprisoned. She found the King and Queen were their normal size again, but very puzzled indeed to find themselves in a cupboard. She quickly explained.

'Call the Captain of the Guard!' the King commanded. 'Have the magician arrested, and his head shall be struck from his shoulders.'

But when the soldiers went to the royal bedchamber to find the false king, they discovered that he was dead, for the moment the Green Ogre had eaten the pear he had perished, as the Wise Woman had predicted.

That day there was great rejoicing in the palace, and Safia went to thank the Wise Woman who lived in the hollow tree. But of the tree there was no sign – it had vanished as if it had never been. Safia could scarcely believe her eyes, and was looking round in a puzzled way when she was approached by a tall, handsome young man, dressed in fine clothes.

'Blessings upon you, dear Princess,' said he, 'for I was the mouse, a victim of enchantment, who nibbled the hole through which you escaped to go upon that journey to find the pear which contained the magician's soul.'

'So it was true, and not a dream!' cried Safia. 'I came to find the Wise Woman and she has gone.'

'She lived in an enchanted tree,' explained the young man, 'and now that she wishes to be elsewhere the tree has been uprooted and taken there without leaving a sign behind.'

'Come with me to my father so that he can thank you,' cried Safia.

So the young man went with her, and when they knelt before the King he explained that he was a prince who had been turned into a mouse by the magician.

'You shall stay here and marry my daughter,' promised the King, 'and rule the kingdom after me, as I have no son.'

And so it came to happen, and the wedding feast was celebrated for seven days and seven nights, and Safia and her husband lived happily ever after.

There they spotted the old man standing stiffly under a tree. They circled him once and made a perfect landing at his feet.

'The goddess Parvati summons you,' they chanted together. Each attendant took one of the old man's hands, lifted him off the ground, and then flew him into the temple's innermost chambers. Parvati was leaning casually against a door, her pale, beautiful face radiating as much light as her gold sari.

'Why are you so unhappy?' she asked gently.

'Praise be to you, goddess,' the old man began as he kneeled and touched her feet, 'I have not eaten for several days.'

'Take this,' said the goddess, handing the old man a simple wooden bowl made from the knot in a teak tree. 'Whenever you are hungry, wash the bowl and pray. Then wish for any food that your heart desires.'

'Any food I want and as *much* as I want?' asked the old man.

'Any food you want and as much as you want,' answered the goddess.

The old man wrapped his precious bowl in rags and began the slow walk home to his wife where they hugged each other, marvelling at Parvati's generosity.

The old man said to his wife, 'Now tell me what you want to eat.'

'How about a sweet mango?'

The old man washed the bowl, prayed and then wished for a sweet mango. Before he could even finish his thought, there was the mango sitting in his bowl.

'What else do you want?' asked the old man.

'How about a rice pilaf made with the meat of a fan-tailed sheep?'

'Here it comes,' said the husband. The bowl was soon brimming over with the fragrant pilaf.

'How about a creamy pudding, dotted with raisins?' ventured the wife.

The wooden bowl was now filled with the tastiest pudding the old couple had ever eaten.

'This is a meal fit for a king,' declared the old man.

'It certainly is,' agreed the wife.

The old man began to think. 'You know,' he started, 'all our lives we have been poor. We have hardly had enough food for ourselves, let alone enough food to entertain guests with. Now that we can have all the finest, rarest delicacies of this world, why don't we invite the King for a meal.'

'You must be mad,' said his wife. 'Why should the King come to eat with the likes of us?'

'And why not?' asked the old man. 'He cannot get a better meal anywhere else. We will be offering the King the best food our heavens can provide.'

So saying, the old man set off to invite the King.

When he arrived at the palace gate, the old man said, 'I have come to invite the King to dinner.'

The guards laughed. 'So you want to invite the King? And why not? This might just make his day.'

They led the old man into the King's chamber thinking that the King would enjoy the joke.

The old man joined his palms and bowed respectfully before the King. 'Your Majesty, I have come to invite you to my home for dinner.'

The King and all his courtiers began to laugh. Some of the courtiers laughed so hard, they practically doubled up from the effort.

'So,' said the King, 'you, ha-ha-ha-ha, want to invite me to, ha-ha-ha-ha, dinner. Do you want me to come alone or do you want my Queen and courtiers as well?'

'Oh, well,' said the old man, 'your Queen and the courtiers are all welcome.'

'Ha-ha-ha-ha,' laughed the whole court.

Now, the King had quite an evil Prime Minister who added his suggestion: 'What about the army? Aren't you going to invite the whole army?'

'Certainly. The whole army is invited as well,' said the old man.

The King and the courtiers laughed so hard, they did not even notice the old man leave.

The day before the dinner, the evil Prime Minister said to the King, 'Your Majesty, would it not be a good idea to check on the old man? Perhaps we should send out some spies to see if dinner for hundreds of thousands is actually being prepared.'

Spies were sent out to the old man's hut. They snooped around for several hours and came back to the palace with this information. 'Your Majesty,' they said, 'we saw a large, neat hut in which enough shiny leaf-plates and earthenware cups were laid out to feed an entire kingdom. But we did not see any signs of food being cooked. No grain was being ground, no rice was soaking and no vegetables were being stewed in pots.'

'Strange. Very strange,' said the King. 'Now that we have accepted the invitation, we will just have to go and see what the old man has in store for us.'

'And if the food is not adequate, we will cut off the old man's head,' the Prime Minister said viciously.

The next day the King, Queen, courtiers and army set off for the old man's hut.

Carpets had been spread on the floor and all the places neatly laid out. There was no sign of food.

The Prime Minister sniffed. 'I cannot smell any kitchen smells. Strange.'

The old man joined his palms together and bowed before the King. 'Please be seated, Your Majesties. It was kind of you to come.' He then washed his wooden bowl and prayed. 'Let the King, Queen, courtiers and army get whatever they desire to eat,' the old man commanded the bowl.

Before anyone could move an eyelid, there appeared muskmelons from Central

Asia, as sweet as sugar, Persian rice pilaf flavoured with saffron and oranges, pheasants and puddings and creams and stews and halvas. As each man and woman dreamt of a particular food, it appeared in the bowl.

The King and his people were amazed. When dinner was finished, the evil Prime Minister turned to the King and said, 'Such an unusual wooden bowl doesn't really belong with this stupid old man. He can eat any old thing. Even scraps. It is you – and your court – who should own this treasure.'

As the King's party was leaving, the evil Prime Minister stretched out his hand, saying, 'The King thanks you for your meal and desires that you let him take care of the bowl.'

What could the old man do? He handed over his bowl – and was left to starve again.

Meanwhile, the King put the old man's bowl into one of his many storerooms and forgot all about it.

When the Nine Days' Festival came around again, the old man returned to Parvati's temple and bowed his head in prayer.

'Oh, goddess Parvati, I made such a mistake. I tried to be so grand. I even invited the King for dinner. Now he has taken the wooden bowl and we are starving.'

Parvati handed the old man a wooden rod and said, 'Take this and whenever you are hungry, wash it, pray and ask for whatever you desire. And do not forget to invite the King to dinner once again.'

The old man did as he was told. He went to the King and asked him to return for another meal. 'Your Majesty, I do hope you will not forget your Queen, courtiers and army.'

This time the King and his courtiers did not laugh. But they were curious. 'I wonder what trick the old man has up his sleeve this time?' mused the evil Prime Minister.

Once again, the King sent spies to the old man's hut a day before the dinner. Once again, the spies returned, saying, 'Your Majesty, we saw a large, neat hut in which enough shining leaf-plates and earthenware cups were laid out to feed an entire kingdom. But we didn't see any signs of food being cooked. No grain was being ground, no rice was soaking and no vegetables were being stirred in pots.'

'Strange. Very strange,' said the King, 'but we have accepted the invitation and must find out what the old man has in store for us.'

The next day the King, Queen, courtiers and army set out for the old man's hut.

The old man put his palms together and bowed before the King and Queen. 'Please be seated, Your Majesties. It was so kind of you to come.' He then washed his wooden rod and prayed. 'Let the King, Queen, courtiers and army get whatever they desire,' he commanded the rod.

But instead of producing food, the rod began flying through the air, beating

everyone. It beat the King, it beat the courtiers, and most of all, it beat the evil Prime Minister.

'Ouch, ouch, ouch,' they all cried.

'Ouch,' cried the evil Prime Minister.

The King turned to the old man. 'Did you call us to dine or did you call us so we could be beaten?' the King asked. 'What is going on here?'

'I beg your forgiveness, Your Majesty,' the old man said. 'I did, indeed, invite you for dinner. The fact of the matter is that this rod is the master and the bowl you have is his wife. The rod is in a bad temper because he wants his wife returned to him.'

The King did not want to be beaten any more so he said to his Prime Minister, 'Where on earth is that wooden bowl we took away from the old man?'

'It is probably lying in some storeroom or other,' said the evil Prime Minister, still rubbing himself all over after his beating.

So the King sent off a servant to his storeroom to find the bowl.

It was only after the bowl was returned to the old man that the beatings stopped.

Then the old man washed both the bowl and rod, prayed and said, 'Let the King, Queen, courtiers and army be served whatever foods they desire.'

The best food from heaven was served.

The old man was happy.

So was his wife.

And so was goddess Parvati.

JAPAN

Traditional

RETOLD BY ERIC QUAYLE

During an early visit to Japan I worked on a book describing the working methods of the most famous artists and craftspeople of the day. This took me to remote areas of the Japanese islands, far from the polluted sprawl of industrial Japan.

These 'Living Treasures' continued to work in the ancient ways of pottery, weaving, sword making, paper making and lacquer work. I was privileged to see this old side of Japan, and the experience was invaluable when I later had an opportunity to illustrate a collection of traditional Japanese stories.

More recently I returned to paint thirty-six views of Mount Fuji, the mountain still managing to appear 'sublime and divine' above the industrial plain. The link which legend makes to the time when man lived closer to nature seems particularly poignant in a crowded country like Japan. Physical links are miniaturised, a stone for a mountain, a bonsai for a tree. But the stories remain epic.

The paper makers house, 1972

My Lord Bag-o'-Rice

In Old Japan, in the far-off days when dragons roamed the land, there lived a brave young warrior named Fujiwara-san who was never happier than when he was waging war against the Emperor's enemies. And this is the story of how he came to change his name.

One day, when travelling alone in the mountains with his bow on his back and his two sharp swords in his belt, he came to the curiously carved bridge of Karashi which spanned one end of the beautiful Lake Biwa. It was a lake famous for the flowering trees which lined its banks and for the snow-capped mountains reflected in its surface.

Fujiwara-san was about to cross the bridge when he noticed that a large serpent was coiled in the middle of the centre arch basking in the warm sunshine. It was the biggest snake he had ever seen, seven or eight metres long at least, and at the young warrior's approach it instantly reared its head. It kept still for a minute then, as Fujiwara-san advanced towards it, it suddenly uncoiled and stretched its length across the bridge in such a way that no one could cross without treading on its scaly body.

Ordinary men would have taken to their heels at so frightening a sight, but Fujiwara-san was no ordinary man. Buckling his sword-belt tighter he strode straight ahead, not pausing for so much as a second as he reached the ugly creature, walking across it with a *crunch! squash! crunch! squash!* before turning and giving it a kick. As he did so it blurted a gush of hot air like a slashed balloon, rapidly becoming smaller and smaller and then disappeared. Where the serpent had been there now crouched a tiny dwarf, a little man of uncertain age who was intent on bowing so low to the young warrior that his head touched the planks of the bridge, not once but three times. Then in a fluting voice the dwarf addressed him in respectful tones, keeping his head held low.

'My Lord! You are a man! A brave and fearless man! I bow my head to you!' And once again his forehead bumped the planks.

Fujiwara-san stood silent, his hand lightly gripping the hilt of the larger of his two swords for trickery was to be expected from any of the magic demons who inhabited this part of the country.

seemed a whole continent was in motion. The thudding and crashing was deafening in his ears, and, as the danger drew nearer, the young warrior could see the monstrous centipede. It was unbelievably huge, an enormous creature a mile or more long. On either side of it there seemed to be a row of a thousand men with lanterns in their hands. Then, as its huge head reached the shores of the lake, Fujiwara-san realised that what he had taken for lines of marching men with lanterns were, in fact, the giant centipede's thousand pairs of feet, all of them glistening and glinting with the sticky poison that oozed from every pore.

There was no time to be lost for the monstrous creature was about to enter the lake. Quick as a flash the young warrior fitted one of his three arrows to the string of the bow, a bow so big and strong that it would have taken three ordinary men to pull it. Taking careful aim with the string at full stretch he let the arrow fly.

He was not one ever to miss his mark, and, sure enough, the arrow struck clean in the middle of the centipede's forehead. To Fujiwara-san's amazement there was a clang and the shaft rebounded! It was as though the monster's head was made of brass!

A second time did our hero take his bow and shoot, and a second time did the arrow find its mark only to glance harmlessly off and ricochet away into the trees.

He had only one arrow left in his quiver. As he fitted the notch to the bow-string he remembered being told by his father when a small boy that centipedes could be killed by human spit. He recalled that he had gone straight out into the garden to spit on one. Sure enough, it had instantly coiled itself into a ball and died. The one

103

in the garden was a few centimetres long, but the beast before him stretched for more than a mile. Would the spittle work?

It had to! It was his only hope! Holding the arrow-head close to his mouth Fujiwara-san spat on it, then let fly the missile just as the centipede raised the first pair of its thousand legs to enter Lake Biwa. Once again the arrow hit the monster in the centre of its forehead, but this time instead of rebounding it penetrated so deeply as to come out at the back of the creature's head. Instantly the centipede reared itself high in the sky, then quivering along its entire length, it keeled over and fell with a crash that shook the earth for miles around. People in villages leagues away rushed out of their houses thinking that an earthquake had taken place and then watched in wonderment as a huge cloud of dust rose into the heavens from the direction of the lake. The centipede was dead, but for an hour or more its feet still glowed and lit up the shoreline. Then one by one they too dimmed and died.

As the light in the last pair of feet was extinguished Fujiwara-san was suddenly whisked off his feet to be transported in seconds back to his own castle. When he opened his eyes it was to find himself in the courtyard surrounded by presents all of which bore labels inscribed with the words 'From your very grateful dwarf'.

The first and much the largest was a dome-shaped bronze bell which our young warrior caused to be hung up in the local temple which contained the tombs of his forbears, for every Japanese man and woman honours the memory of their ancestors.

He was very pleased with the second of the Dragon King's presents, a magic sword whose edge could as easily cut through stone or steel as it could a floating feather. With this and his third present, a suit of armour which no arrow could penetrate, there was no way he could be vanquished by jealous enemies.

Label number four was tied to a bolt of the most expensive and finest silk, a roll of material which had the ability to change colour and design as the mood took him, and which, no matter how many times his wife cut off large or small pieces for yet another kimono or for a new court dress for her Master, never became any less. The roll always remained the same length as though it had not been touched, so that Fujiwara-san often had clothes made for poor people and their children and his name was blessed throughout the land.

But it was the fifth present that gave him the most joy. It was a large bag of best quality rice, which, though the family scooped measures from it every day for meals for themselves and their trusty retainers, remained always full. It never diminished in quantity so that Fujiwara-san was always able to feed the poor and needy.

Within weeks he was being referred to as 'My Lord Bag-o'-Rice', words spoken with the utmost respect and always with a low bow of the head. He and his family were loved throughout Old Japan and he finally died a venerated saint and a rich and happy man.

CHINA

Traditional

China has a longer legacy of written stories than any other culture, some 3,000 years. Chinese mythology dates from an even more remote past and some of the stories reflect the very creation of the landscape which in turn shapes the lives of the people to this day.

When I travelled around China in the early 1970s, thousands of men and women were working in the flood plains of the rivers constructing dikes, dams and pumping stations to harness the power and avoid the disastrous floods of the past. In the previous 400 years the Yellow River alone has flooded 1,500 times and changed course six times.

The awesome yet essential power of the great rivers of China is reflected in the story of 'The Four Dragons'.

Four old men. Northern China 1974

The Four Dragons

Long, long ago in the beginning of time, there were no rivers and lakes on the earth, only the vast Eastern Sea, in which lived four dragons: the Long Dragon, the Yellow Dragon, the Black Dragon and the Pearl Dragon.

One day the four dragons flew from the sea up to the sky, and chased and dived among the clouds. Suddenly the Pearl Dragon roared and pointed to the earth. The other three dragons gathered round and peered through the clouds in the direction the Pearl Dragon pointed.

They saw many people placing special offerings on the ground, and burning incense sticks. An old woman, kneeling on the bare earth with a thin little boy in her arms cried, 'God of Heaven, please send rain so our children may live.'

The dragons saw that the rice fields were dry, the crops withered, and the leafless trees stood about like skeletons. There had obviously been no rain for a very long time.

'How thin and weak the people are' said the Yellow Dragon. 'They will die if it doesn't rain soon.' The other dragons nodded.

'Let us go and ask the Jade Emperor for Rain.' suggested the Long Dragon and soared up from the clouds and flew towards the distant sky palace of the Jade Emperor.

The all-powerful Jade Emperor was not at all pleased by the unceremonious arrival of the dragons. 'How dare you interrupt my important business of taking care of Heaven and Earth and all else besides. Get back to the sea and behave yourselves!'

'But Your Majesty, the crops on earth are dying, and the people are starving,' said the Long Dragon, 'Please send down rain quickly.'

The Jade Emperor wanted to get back to his day dreams, so he pretended to agree. 'Oh alright.' he said, 'You go back now, and I will send rain tomorrow.'

'Thank you Your Majesty!' chorused the four dragons, and flew happily back to Earth. The Jade Emperor signalled to a thousand sky fairies to sing his favourite lullaby, yawned, and fell asleep.

Ten days passed, and not a drop of rain came down. The people grew more and more hungry. They ate the withered grass, nibbled the dry limbs of the trees, sucked stones and chewed the dry clay.

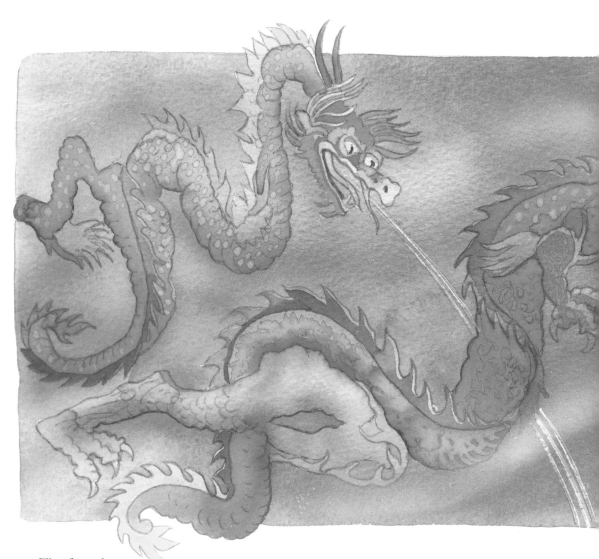

The four dragons realized the Jade Emperor thought only of his own pleasure, and cared nothing for the people. Then, after gazing at the vast Eastern Sea, the Long Dragon had an idea. 'Is not the sea full of water? We must suck it up and spray it towards the sky. It will fall like rain and save the crops and the people.'

The other dragons agreed they had to try something, and this idea was the only one they had.

They flew over the sea and scooped up water in their mouths. Then they soared back above the clouds and sprayed water all around. The dragons flew back and forth many times, scooping and spraying, scooping and spraying until the sea water fell as rain.

'It's raining! It's pouring!' the people cried with joy and children splashed about in the puddles. Rivulets trickled, then gushed over the cracked rice fields, and green shoots raised their heads to the falling rain.

The Jade Emperor was furious, and ordered his sky generals to capture the four dragons.

'How dare you make rain without my permission!' he raged when the dragons were brought before him. 'You have disobeyed me for the last time.'

He commanded the Mountain God to bring four mountains to be placed on the dragons so they could never escape again. The Mountain God caused four far away mountains to fly through the air and land on the four dragons.

So there the dragons had to remain, weighed down by mountains forever.

However they had no regrets and were more determined than ever to help the local people. They turned themselves into rivers, flowing from the mountains across the now fertile land to the sea.

And so China's four great rivers were formed: the Heilongjiang (the Black Dragon) in the cold far north, the Huanghe (Yellow River) in the centre, the Changjiang (Yangtze or Long River) further south and the Zhujiang (Pearl) in the far and tropical south.

MEXICO

Traditional

When the Spanish conquistadores arrived in the New World they found a spectacular old world. There had already been six distinct civilisations in Mexico culminating with the Aztec.

The Aztec capital (Tenochtitlan) was built on islands in a vast lake. It was destroyed by the Spanish and the beginnings of Mexico City built amid the ruins. Today it is necessary to travel to remote areas of Mexico and the Yucatan peninsula to see something of the scale and splendour that Tenochtitlan must have had.

But Popocatepetl, the Smoking Mountain, broods over modern Mexico City, and reminds the citizens of a rich and violent past.

This story tells of a great hero and how the mountain got its name.

The Castillo
Chichen-Itza, Yucatan.
Michael Foreman.

mexico 1977

Popocatepetl and the Princess

Long ago, in ancient Mexico, there lived a powerful Emperor. He had a fine city built, set about with gardens and ringed by fertile fields.

He and the Empress lived in great splendour, but it was not until they were in their middle years that they finally achieved that which they had most longed for – a child.

The Emperor and Empress loved their little princess dearly, and she was their only child. They named her Ixtlaccihuatl, or Ixtla for short.

As she grew up she learned all she could from her father for she knew that when he died she would take his place as ruler of the great city of Tenochtitlan.

She grew to become a truly beautiful princess, but despite the richness and privileges of her life her father denied her one thing. He forbad her to marry. He wanted her to rule alone when he died, as he trusted no one but his beloved daughter.

But Ixtla was already in love with a young warrior called Popocatepetl who was in the service of her father.

Several times the young lovers pleaded with the Emperor to let them marry but he always refused.

The years passed and the Emperor became old and feeble. His enemies who lived in the surrounding mountains realized the great Emperor was great no longer. They swept down from the mountains and besieged the city.

The Emperor knew that if his enemies were not defeated, not only would he lose his power, but his daughter would never become Empress. He was too old to lead his warriors into battle, but he did not wish to appoint one man to lead the rest. Instead he offered the hand of his daughter in marriage to the warrior who was the most brave and successful in lifting the siege and driving the enemy back to the mountains.

The warriors were delighted by this plan, for all of them would love to have the Princess as a wife, and the chance of eventually becoming Emperor. Ixtla, however, was very upset as there was only one man she wished to marry – Popocatepetl.

And so the warriors attacked the surrounding city and each fought doubly hard to save their city and to win the Princess and the right to be Emperor.

The war was long and terrible, but eventually Popocatepetl was seen to be the natural leader, and it was he who led the final great charge which drove the enemy back beyond the mountains and far from Tenochtitlan. Popocatepetl was cheered by the other warriors as the man most responsible for the victory. But some of the warriors were jealous and slipped away from the rest at night and journeyed back to the city ahead of the others.

The Emperor was anxious to hear news of the war and the group of jealous warriors told how they had won a famous victory, but added that unfortunately Popocatepetl had been killed in the final battle.

The old Emperor was saddened to hear this. He knew the man his daughter loved would have died bravely. He asked which of his warriors had been most responsible for the victory. The jealous warriors looked at one another and knew they could never agree on which of them had been most brave, so they said nothing. This puzzled the Emperor and he decided to wait until the rest of his army returned.

But he sent for his wife and the Princess and told them of the defeat of their enemies, and the sad death of Popocatepetl.

The Princess went to her room and lay down. Her mother saw at once that she was very ill. Witch doctors were called, but they had no cure for a broken heart. Princess Ixtla had no wish to live if Popocatepetl was dead, so she died herself.

The next day Popocatepetl and the victorious army returned to the city in triumph. There was much cheering as they made their way to the palace. The Emperor was at last told the true story of the battle and that Popocatepetl had been the great leader.

The old Emperor praised his warriors and declared Popocatepetl to be the new Emperor in his place. Popocatepetl was amazed to hear this.

'But Your Majesty, all I desire is to marry your daughter.'

The old Emperor then had to tell of Princess Ixtla's death, and how it happened.

Popotatepetl said not a word, but turned and sought out the jealous men who had brought the false news of his death. He killed each one in single combat with his studded club. Then he returned to the palace and still without saying a word, went to Ixtla's room, gently lifted her body and carried her from the palace and out of the city. All the warriors and all the people of the city followed him in silence.

When they had walked some miles, and at a sign from Popocatepetl, they began to build a huge mound of stones in the shape of a pyramid. The whole population worked together.

By sunset the mighty work was finished. Popocatepetl climbed it alone, Princess Ixtla still cradled in his arms. At the very top he buried his love under a heap of stones. He sat alone at the top of the pyramid as the sky turned from blood red to the black of night.

When the sun returned to the valley, he came down and asked the warriors to build a second pyramid a little to the south east, and to build it higher than the other. He said he had no wish to be Emperor and wanted only to watch over the grave of Princess Ixtla for the rest of his life.

When the second pyramid was finished Popocatepetl climbed to the top and lit a torch of sweet smelling resinous pine. The people below watched the white smoke rise against the changing colours of the sky. And so Popocatepetl stood, holding the torch in memory of the Princess who died for love of him.

The snows came, and as the years went by, the pyramids became high, white-capped mountains. Eventually the Spanish came to Mexico and destroyed much of the beautiful Tenochtitlan and built another city in its place, which became Mexico City.

From Mexico City today you can see two beautiful snow-capped mountains. One is called Ixtlaccihuatl in memory of Princess Ixtla. The other, taller, mountain is called Popocatepetl and a plume of white smoke still climbs from the peak into the Mexican sky.

little dance and fired off a whole flight of spines at the clouds. Still the sun did not appear.

Then a gruff old bear got *really* angry. He stormed to the top of the hill and shook both fists at the sky, trying to think of the most threatening thing to shout at the sun. He was so angry and flustered that he could think of nothing terrible enough. All the crowd tried to think of what the bear should shout at the sun, and the bear jumped up and down in his rage.

Just then, a bat who had been sleeping soundly throughout the proceedings, woke up. He had missed the red bird's song, the bonfire, the arrows and the porcupines spines, but he had enjoyed a very lovely dream, and he smiled an enormous beaming smile.

Bats, as you know, sleep upside down, and when the crowd saw the bat's hilarious upside down smile they couldn't help laughing. Even the gruff old bear giggled and then fell to the ground helpless with laughter. The laughter rolled around the valley, and the sun, hearing the noise, parted the clouds slightly and looked down. The thin beam of sunlight fell upon the little bat and his wide upside down smile.

The sun burst out laughing, and his laughter drove away the clouds. The people and animals saw the sun beaming from the mountain tops and then climb once more into the sky.

GERMANY

The Brothers Grimm

RETOLD BY BRIAN ALDERSON

In the days of the travelling storyteller, everyday objects, tools, sieves, stools, bowls, would be made within the household, or by a neighbour. They were valued and individual. Such objects were often central to a traditional story. They helped make stories familiar, real. The incidents had to be marvellous, but the human situation needed to be recognisable. The spindle is the centre around which the story of Sleeping Beauty revolves.

When Jacob and Wilhelm Grimm began collecting stories the great forests were still very much part of the real world. The stories they heard grew from the old folklore of the forest. Such stories, distilled by generations of re-telling, convey the deepest wishes of ordinary people.

They tell of the past that is inside us. The past which is outside is History. The past inside lives.

Briar-Rose or, The Sleeping Beauty

Once upon a time there was a king and a queen who longed with all their hearts to have a child, but they couldn't get one. Then, one day, while the Queen was bathing, a crab crept out of the water on to the bank and said, 'Your wish shall be fulfilled. Soon you shall bring a daughter into the world.' And the crab was right. A princess was born, and the King was so full of joy that he had a great feast prepared and asked all the fairies in the land to come. (Now you must know that there were thirteen of these fairies, but because the King had only twelve golden plates one of them wasn't invited.)

Well, the fairies came to the feast, and when it was over they gave the child their gifts: the first, virtue, the second, beauty, and so on with the others – everything in the world that anyone would wish for. But just as the eleventh fairy had said her blessing, the thirteenth one marched in, all fury that she hadn't been invited. 'Because you did not bid me come,' she cried, 'I tell you that your daughter will, in her fifteenth year, prick herself on a spindle and fall down dead.' The King and queen were horrified; but the twelfth fairy still had a gift to offer, and she said: 'This shall be no death. The Princess shall only fall into a deep sleep for a hundred years.'

Despite all this, the King still hoped to save his darling daughter and he sent out the command that all the spindles in the whole kingdom should be done away with.

So it was then that the Princess grew up, a perfect miracle of beauty. One day, though, when she had just reached her fifteenth year, the King and Queen had gone out and she was left all by herself in the castle. She wandered about, here, there and everywhere, just as she wanted to until at last she came to an old tower. There was a narrow staircase leading into it and, since she was inquisitive, she climbed up it until she came to a little door with a yellow key in the lock. This she turned and the door sprang open and she found herself in a tiny little room, with an old woman sitting there spinning her flax.

'Good day to you, little mother,' said the Princess, 'what are you doing?'

'I am spinning,' said the old woman, and nodded her head.

'And what's this thing bobbing about here?' asked the Princess, and took the spindle to try it; but hardly had she touched it then she pricked her finger with it and straightaway fell into a deep sleep.

At that moment the King returned with all his court and every one of them began to fall asleep; the horses in the stables and the pigeons on the roof, the dogs in the courtyard and the flies on the wall, yes, even the fire in the hearth flickered, died down and slept, and the roasting meat stopped spitting and the cook let go the kitchen-boy, whose hair he was going to pull, and the maid let fall the fowl she was plucking and fell asleep. And around the whole castle there sprang up a hedge of thorns, higher and higher, so that you couldn't see any of it any more.

Even so, there were princes who had heard of the lovely Princess Briar-Rose and who came determined to free her. But they could force no way through the hedge. It was as though the thorns held fast together like claws and the princes were caught up among them and died a miserable death.

In this way the long, long years went by until one day a king's son was travelling through the land. An old man told him how people believed that a castle stood behind the hedge of thorns with a beautiful princess sleeping there and all her court. He said his grandfather had told him how many a prince had come in times past, seeking to force a way through, but how they'd all been caught up in the thorns and pricked to death.

'That's not something to scare me,' said the King's son. 'I'll get through the hedge and set the beautiful Briar-Rose free,' and he went off.

When he came to the hedge of thorns it changed to blossoming flowers, which parted to let him through, and turned to thorns behind him again. Then he came to the castle, and in the courtyard the horses lay sleeping, and the brindled hunting-dogs, and on the roof the pigeons sat with their heads tucked under their wings. And, when he entered the building, the flies were sleeping on the wall, and the fire in the kitchen-hearth, and the cook still held up his hand to clout the kitchen-boy, and the maid still had the old black hen in front of her. So he went further, and there lay the royal court sleeping, and further still, there were the King and Queen – and everything was so quiet that he could hear himself breathing.

At last he came to the old tower and there, at the top, lay the Princess Briar-Rose, sleeping. And the king's son was so amazed at her beauty that he bent down and kissed her, and in that moment she awoke. Then too the King and Queen awoke and their courtiers, looking at each other in astonishment, and the horses shook themselves, and the dogs jumped about and wagged their tails, and the pigeons on the roof took their heads out from under their wings, looked around, and flew off to the fields, and the flies on the wall began to crawl again, and the fire sprang up and flared and finished cooking the dinner; the roast went on spitting and the cook boxed the kitchen-boy's ears and the maid plucked all the feathers from the hen.

Then the marriage was celebrated between Briar-Rose and the King's son and they lived happily to the end of their days.

DENMARK

Hans Christian Andersen

RETOLD BY ERIK HAUGAARD

In the late 1960s I made six animated films in Denmark. I lived on a farm with friends and the whole household helped paint the drawings for the films. After work in the summertime we played hide and seek in the fields and overgrown orchard. After work in the wintertime it was time for stories. The little farmhouse, the animals, the children and the turning seasons seemed pure Hans Andersen.

Andersen was born in Odense, Denmark in 1805. The son of a shoemaker, his stories brought him great fame and his house in Odense is now the Hans Christian Andersen Museum.

The story of Inchelina has many of the classic ingredients. A closely observed and recognisable world, the tiny child, a series of close encounters opening out into the best ingredient of all – a fabulous journey.

H.C. Andersens childhood home   Odense Denmark.

Inchelina

Once upon a time there was a woman whose only desire was to have a tiny little child. Now she had no idea where she could get one; so she went to an old witch and asked her: 'Please, could you tell me where I could get a tiny little child? I would so love to have one.'

'That is not so difficult,' said the witch. 'Here is a grain of barley; it is not the kind that grows in the farmer's fields or that you can feed to the chickens. Plant it in a flowerpot and watch what happens.'

'Thank you,' said the woman. She handed the witch twelve pennies, and she went home to plant the grain of barley. No sooner was it in the earth than it started to sprout. A beautiful big flower grew up; it looked like a tulip that was just about to bloom.

'What a lovely flower,' said the woman, and kissed the red and yellow petals that were closed so tightly. With a snap they opened and one could see that it was a real tulip. In the centre of the flower on the green stigma sat a tiny little girl. She was so beautiful and so delicate, and exactly one inch long. 'I will call her Inchelina,' thought the woman.

The lacquered shell of a walnut became Inchelina's cradle, the blue petals of violets her mattress, and a rose petal her cover. Here she slept at night; in the daytime she played on the table by the window. The woman had put a bowl of water there with a garland of flowers around it. In this tiny 'lake' there floated a tulip petal, on which Inchelina could row from one side of the plate to the other, using two white horsehairs as oars; it was an exquisite sight. And Inchelina could sing, as no one has ever sung before – so clearly and delicately.

One night as she lay sleeping in her beautiful little bed a toad came into the room through a broken windowpane. The toad was big and wet and ugly; she jumped down upon the table where Inchelina was sleeping under her red rose petal.

'She would make a lovely wife for my son,' said the toad; and grabbing the walnut shell in which Inchelina slept, she leaped through the broken window and down into the garden.

On the banks of a broad stream, just where it was muddiest, lived the toad with her son. He had taken after his mother and was very ugly. 'Croak . . . Croak . . .

Croak!' was all he said when he saw the beautiful little girl in the walnut shell.

'Don't talk so loud or you will wake her,' scolded the mother. 'She could run away and we wouldn't be able to catch her, for she is as light as the down of a swan. I will put her on a water-lily leaf, it will be just like an island to her. In the meantime, we shall get your house, down in the mud, ready for your marriage.'

Out in the stream grew many water lilies, and all of their leaves looked as if they were floating in the water. The biggest of them was the farthest from shore; on that one the old toad put Inchelina's little bed.

When the poor little girl woke in the morning and saw where she was – on a green leaf with water all around her – she began to cry bitterly. There was no way of getting to shore at all.

The old toad was very busy down in her mud house, decorating the walls with reeds and yellow flowers that grew near the shore. She meant to do her best for her new daughter-in-law. After she had finished, she and her ugly son swam out to the water-lily leaf to fetch Inchelina's bed. It was to be put in the bridal chamber. The old toad curtsied and that is not easy to do while you are swimming; then she said, 'Here is my son. He is to be your husband; you two will live happily down in the mud.'

'Croak! . . . Croak! . . .' was all the son said. Then they took the bed and swam away with it. Poor Inchelina sat on the green leaf and wept and wept, for she did not want to live with the ugly toad and have her hideous son as a husband. The little fishes that were swimming about in the brook had heard what the old toad said; they stuck their heads out of the water to take a look at the tiny girl. When they saw how beautiful she was, it hurt them to think that she should have to marry the ugly toad and live in the mud. They decided that they would not let it happen, and gathered around the green stalk that held the leaf anchored to the bottom of the stream. They all nibbled on the stem, and soon the leaf was free. It drifted down the stream, bearing Inchelina far away from the ugly toad.

As Inchelina sailed by, the little birds on the shore saw her and sang, 'What a lovely little girl.' Farther and farther sailed the leaf with its little passenger, taking her on a journey to foreign lands.

For a long time a lovely white butterfly flew around her, then landed on the leaf. It had taken a fancy to Inchelina. The tiny girl laughed, for she was so happy to have escaped the toad; and the stream was so beautiful, golden in the sunshine. She took the little silk ribbon which she wore around her waist and tied one end of it to the butterfly and the other to the water-lily leaf. Now the leaf raced down the stream – and so did Inchelina, for she was standing on it.

At that moment a big May bug flew by; when it spied Inchelina, it swooped down and with its claws grabbed the poor girl around her tiny waist and flew up into a tree with her. The leaf floated on down the stream, and the buttertfly had to follow it.

Oh God, little Inchelina was terrified as the May bug flew away with her, but stronger than her fear was her grief for the poor little white butterfly that she had chained to the leaf with her ribbon. If he did not get loose, he would starve to death.

The May bug didn't care what happened to the butterfly. He placed Inchelina on the biggest leaf on the tree. He gave her honey from the flowers to eat, and told her that she was the loveliest thing he had ever seen, even though she didn't look like a May bug. Soon all the other May bugs that lived in the tree came visiting. Two young lady May bugs – they were still unmarried – wiggled their antennae and said: 'She has only two legs, how wretched! No antennae and a thin waist, how disgusting! She looks like a human being: how ugly!'

All the other female May bugs agreed with them. The May bug who had caught Inchelina still thought her lovely; but when all the others kept insisting that she was ugly, he soon was convinced of it too. Now he didn't want her any longer, and put her down on a daisy at the foot of the tree and told her she could go wherever she wanted to, for all he cared. Poor Inchelina cried; she thought it terrible to be so ugly that even a May bug would not want her, and that in spite of her being more beautiful than you can imagine, more lovely than the petal of the most beautiful rose.

All summer long poor Inchelina lived all alone in the forest. She wove a hammock out of grass and hung it underneath a dock leaf so that it would not rain on her while she slept. She ate the honey in the flowers and drank the dew that was on their leaves every morning.

Summer and autumn passed. But then came winter: the long, cold winter. All the birds that had sung so beautifully flew away. The flowers withered, the trees lost their leaves; and the dock leaf that had protected her rolled itself up and became a shrivelled yellow stalk. She was so terribly cold. Her clothes were in shreds; and she was so thin and delicate.

Poor Inchelina, she was bound to freeze to death. It started to snow and each snowflake that fell on her was like a whole shovelful of snow would be to us, because we are so big, and she was only one inch tall.

She wrapped herself in a wizened leaf, but it gave no warmth and she shivered from the cold.

Not far from the forest was a big field where grain had grown; only a few dry stubbles still rose from the frozen ground, pointing up to the heavens. To Inchelina these straws were like a forest. Trembling, she wandered through them and came to the entrance of a field mouse's house. It was only a little hole in the ground. But deep down below the mouse lived in warmth and comfort, with a full larder and a nice kitchen. Like a beggar child, Inchelina stood outside the door and begged for a single grain of barley. It was several days since she had last eaten.

'Poor little wretch,' said the field mouse, for she had a kind heart. 'Come down into my warm living room and dine with me.'

132

The field mouse liked Inchelina. 'You can stay the winter,' she said, 'But you must keep the room tidy and tell me a story every day, for I like a good story.' Inchelina did what the kind old mouse demanded, and she lived quite happily.

'Soon we shall have a visitor,' said the mouse. 'Once a week my neighbour comes. He lives even more comfortably than I do. He has a drawing room, and wears the most exquisite black fur coat. If only he would marry you, then you would be well provided for. He can't see you, for he is blind, so you will have to tell him the very best of your stories.'

But Inchelina did not want to marry the mouse's neighbour, for he was a mole. The next day he came visiting, dressed in his black velvet fur coat. The field mouse said that he was both rich and wise. His house was twenty times as big as hers, and he was cultured, too. But he did not like the sun nor the beautiful flowers, he said they were 'abominable,' for he had never seen them. Inchelina had to sing for him; and when she sang *'Frère Jacques, dormez vous?'* he fell in love with her because of her beautiful voice; but he didn't show it, for he was sober-minded and never made a spectacle of himself.

He had recently dug a passage from his own house to theirs, and he invited Inchelina and the field mouse to use it as often as they pleased. He told them not to be afraid of the dead bird in the corridor. It had died only a few days before. It was still whole and had all its feathers. By chance it had been buried in his passageway.

The mole took a piece of dry rotten wood in his mouth; it shone as brightly as fire in the darkness; then he led the way down through the long corridor. When they came to the place where the dead bird lay, the mole made a hole with his broad nose, up through the earth, so that light could come through. Almost blocking the passageway was a dead swallow, with its beautiful wings pressed close to its body, its feet almost hidden by feathers, and its head nestled under a wing. The poor bird undoubtedly had frozen to death. Inchelina felt a great sadness; she had loved all the birds that twittered and sang for her that summer. The mole kicked the bird with one of his short legs and said, 'Now it has stopped chirping. What a misfortune it is to be born a bird. Thank God, none of my children will be born birds! All they can do is chirp, and then die of starvation when winter comes.'

'Yes, that's what all sensible people think,' said the field mouse. 'What does all that chirping lead to? Starvation and cold when winter comes. But I suppose they think it is romantic.'

Inchelina didn't say anything, but when the mouse and mole had their backs turned, she leaned down and kissed the closed eye of the swallow. 'Maybe that was one of the birds that sang so beautifully for me this summer,' she thought. 'How much joy you gave me, beautiful little bird.'

The mole closed the hole through which the daylight had entered and then escorted the ladies home. That night Inchelina could not sleep; she rose and wove as large a blanket as she could, out of hay. She carried it down the dark passage and covered the little bird with it. In the field mouse's living room she had found bits of cotton; she tucked them under the swallow wherever she could, to protect it from the cold earth.

'Good-bye, beautiful bird,' she said. 'Good-bye, and thank you for the songs you sang for me when it was summer and all the trees were green and the sun warmed us.'

She put her head on the bird's breast; then she jumped up! Something was ticking inside: it was the bird's heart, for the swallow was not really dead, and now the warmth had revived it.

In the autumn all the swallows fly to the warm countries. If one tarries too long and is caught by the first frost, he lies down on the ground as if he were dead, and the cold snow covers him.

Inchelina shook with fear. The swallow was huge to a girl so tiny that she only measured an inch. But she gathered her courage and pressed the blanket closer to the bird's body. She even went to fetch the little mint leaf that she herself used as a cover and put it over the bird's head.

The next night she sneaked down to the passageway again; the bird was better although still very weak. He opened his eyes just long enough to see Inchelina standing in the dark with a little piece of rotten wood in her hand, as a lamp.

They came to the warm countries. And it was true what the swallow had said: the sun shone more brightly and the sky seemed twice as high. Along the fences grew the loveliest green and blue grapes. From the trees in the forests hung oranges and lemons. Along the roads the most beautiful children ran, chasing many-coloured butterflies. The swallow flew even farther south, and the landscape beneath them became more and more beautiful.

Near a forest, on the shores of a lake, stood the ruins of an ancient temple; ivy wound itself around the white pillars. On top of these were many swallows' nests and one of them belonged to the little swallow that was carrying Inchelina.